LANDON'S

the power of a brief life

LEGACY

Dear Kerrie,

May you find comfort &
hope in Landon's story.

xo Amelia Barnes

AMELIA KATHRYN BARNES

First Printing 2016

PRINTED IN THE UNITED STATES OF AMERICA

Book and cover design by Kerri-lynn Wilkinson
Cover photography by Amelia Kathryn Barnes

For Landon.

Thank you for being my inspiration

and my guiding light.

I love you.

The deeper that sorrow carves into your being, the more joy you can contain... When you are joyous, look deep into your heart and you shall find it is only that which has given you sorrow that is giving you joy. When you are sorrowful look again in your heart, and you shall see that in truth you are weeping for that which has been your delight.

—KHALIL GIBRAN, *THE PROPHET*

INTRODUCTION

On July 8th, 2014, I gave birth to our son, Landon James Barnes. He was 8 pounds 6 ounces and 21 inches of pure perfection—the most beautiful newborn I have ever laid eyes on. Four days later, my husband and I held our baby son as his spirit left his little body. With his silky-soft skin pressed against my bare chest, I could feel every raspy breath, every faint heartbeat as they slowed and then stopped completely. What should have been the most joyful point in my life became the most sorrowful.

This is the story of that first year and a half following the birth and death of our son, based on a compilation of journal entries that I shared on my Instagram account, @ameliakyoga, between June 2014 and November 2015. As a yoga teacher and practitioner, as well as the owner of a small yoga-apparel business, I had begun posting photos of my yoga practice, clothing and other aspects of my life shortly before I found out I was pregnant with Landon. I experienced tremendous support and inspiration in the Instagram yoga community and, therefore, continued documenting my yoga practice and my journey through pregnancy.

Before Landon was born, I never kept a journal, and I never wrote much online other than those brief updates near the end of my pregnancy. When Landon's death catapulted me into an intensity of emotional and physical pain beyond my imagining, writing became an integral part of my day-to-day survival. I clung to my phone for months just so I could write down my thoughts as they swept through my mind in a tornado of grief, anger and despair. Writing helped to clean up some of the wreckage; it helped me organize my thoughts and make sense of things again.

At first I was hesitant to share my writing online. I was afraid of the hurtful, judgmental things people might say. I knew I was in a vulnerable place and it would take a thick skin to go public with what is generally considered a private affair, a silent grief—the loss of a baby during pregnancy or shortly after birth. But I knew I couldn't be silent. I felt deep in my freshly ripped-open heart that Landon's brief life was meant to be something bigger. His story needed to be heard.

As it turns out, writing, sharing photos and connecting with the online community of bereaved parents was my saving grace. Social media became my journal, my lifeline and, at times, my only real connection to the outside world. It helped me immeasurably to have Landon's life recognized. It filled me with pride to have others know his name and admire his precious face. I realized very quickly that infant loss is far more common than I once thought and that being able to connect with other parents also going through this tragedy helped me feel less isolated and alone. Especially during the first few months after Landon's death, that connection gave me a reason to get out of bed each day, a reason to keep moving forward. It also gave me a means to show off Landon, seeing that in everyday life it's rare that people ask or want to hear about your dead baby. In a sense, social media became my way of mothering my son.

I also saw how much my writing helped others. The responses I received were truly incredible. In the year following Landon's passing, my online following grew from 10,000 to over 100,000, and I've had the honour of seeing my son's little life make an impact in a big way. Through my social media accounts, people facing all kinds of losses and life struggles come together for support and inspiration and to share their experiences. My connection with this community of others also gave me the inspiration to create a healing yoga retreat for bereaved mothers in June 2015.

SUMMER

waiting for landon

JUNE 20

I realized I haven't posted anything in a while. Actually, my husband, Justin, said to me today, "Why don't you take some photos? I miss seeing your updates."

So, here I am! With baby arriving any day now, I've decided to start writing down my thoughts and experiences. I've never really kept a journal before. (The few attempts I made as a pre-teen lasted only ever a few days.) These days of waiting have my mind spinning with anticipation, though, and I need a way to sort through my emotions. I also think it will be nice to document this momentous time in my life so that one day I can look back and read about this amazing adventure that baby and I have been on.

Today I spent some time working in our yard. It was a long, cold winter (one of the coldest in history), so the green grass and flowers have only recently pushed their way up through the earth. I'm pretty happy with how well my garden is doing considering its late start. I get very excited about my lilies in particular. They are incredibly beautiful when in bloom, which is only for a few weeks in late June and early July. I took some photos of them today—there are no blooms yet, but it looks like there will be soon. Thank you all for your kind words and the guesses on baby's arrival day and weight. And here's my prediction—our baby will be born on the day my lilies come into full bloom!

JUNE 22

Tomorrow my baby is thirty-nine weeks! At first I thought I wouldn't enjoy being pregnant, but now I think I will miss it when it's over. There are so many things I love about being pregnant—I love how I now wake up every morning and admire how much bigger my belly has gotten, rather than pinching loose skin and wishing for a six-pack. I also find I intuitively want to eat healthy, fresh, whole foods—junk food and anything processed just tastes gross! And because baby is taking up so much space, I have to eat smaller meals more regularly, which make my energy levels and digestion much better.

But most of all, I love feeling baby's movements. His legs and bum are always bulging out in interesting ways, and he likes to tickle me with his tiny fingers. I think he's going to be an energetic boy, just like his dad. But as much as I'm enjoying being pregnant, I really can't wait to meet our little boy. I keep dreaming of what it will be like to hold him in my arms and look into to his sweet newborn eyes, to feel his soft skin and count all his fingers and toes. I never knew it was possible to love someone this much.

JULY 6

Today I'm feeling more grateful than ever for my husband. I remember clearly that six years ago when we were on our first date I decided I wanted Justin to be the father of my children. I even went home and told my mom that I'd met the guy I was going to marry. There was something about the way he wholeheartedly and unconditionally cared for the loved ones in his life that made me sure. To this day, he is my rock and the best dad in the world to our dog Cody (our "first child"). It fills my heart with joy that we will be meeting our baby boy any day now. The last few days of anticipation haven't been the easiest, but Justin is always there to remind me of how strong I am.

JULY 7

Well, baby sure is taking his sweet time! I'm forty-one weeks pregnant today. We had a fetal assessment this morning and everything looks great—baby is healthy, has plenty of amniotic fluid and looks to be around seven pounds. The doctors say that it's common for first-time moms to go a week or two past their due dates, so I'm trying to relax as much as I can and let my body do what it needs to do. As excited and impatient as I am to meet our little guy, I'm also finding there is something special about these final days. I know that soon life will change in many amazing ways, but right now I'm trying to stay present and connected to each magical moment.

This evening I enjoyed a relaxing prenatal yoga class and then went for a long walk around the Forks with my friend Trinette. I took some photos of the Provencher Bridge, which looked particularly beautiful at sunset. I have a feeling baby is coming very soon.

meeting our son landon

JULY 10

It's 3 a.m. I keep waking up thinking I'm trapped in a crazy nightmare. Just over twenty-four hours ago we met our baby boy, Landon James. After about eight hours of labour, I was eight centimetres dilated. Suddenly his heartbeat dropped dangerously low, and I was rushed into the operating room for an emergency C-section. By the time they got him out, it was too late. His heart had stopped beating. It took over fifteen minutes to resuscitate him, and by that time his brain was severely damaged. No one knows exactly what happened. The doctors and nurses seem to be in as much shock as we are. He is still on life support, but it's not looking good. We are praying for a miracle.

The last twenty-four hours have been more emotionally and physically painful than I could ever imagine. Nothing in my life could have prepared me for this. Part of me wants to curl up in my hospital bed, disappear and never have to face the real world again. But at the same time I'm overwhelmed by gratitude—for my husband and my dad who have been with Landon every moment while I recover; for my mom and doula who massage my body that has completely seized up; and for my sister who helps me move and manage the excruciating pain and holds me in her arms at night until I fall asleep. I can't remember what life was like before this nightmare began; I can't imagine what it will be like from now on. The present moment is too hard to bear. Everything hurts, just hurts.

It's 7 p.m., forty-two hours since Landon was born. I still feel as though I'm stuck in a nightmare that I can't wake up from. Time is moving so, so slowly. Sometimes it seems that the minute hand on the clock isn't moving at all. Nothing feels real. Landon doesn't even feel real. I was under general anesthesia when he was rushed to the Neonatal Intensive Care Unit (NICU), and he took so long to be stabilized that

I didn't get to see him for what seemed like a lifetime. I know he's ours because he looks just like me, with his round face and button nose. Still, it's hard to believe that this baby is the same one who was so lively and healthy inside of me only a few days ago.

While today was much harder because the numbing effect of all the drugs in me is wearing off, there were also some good things. I got discharged early from the Women's Hospital so I could move to the NICU. Justin and I got a beautifully furnished room (with a king-size bed) that's reserved for the parents of the most critical NICU babies. I'm able to spend more time with Landon now that I can sit and even stand longer, and I've been pumping colostrum and using it for cleaning his mouth, even though he can't eat. Also, I did get to change his diaper after he passed his first meconium today. I never thought changing my baby's dirty diaper could be the highlight of my day, but it was. Doing that for him made me feel at least a bit like a normal mom.

The hardest thing right now is not being able to hold my son because of all the tubes he's hooked up to. It feels unnatural, so wrong, to be separated from him, not to be able to comfort him. He has been a part of me ever since he was conceived. I feel as though I've abandoned him in a way, and it breaks my heart to not know how much, if anything, he can sense. Does he hear my voice, know my touch and my smell or long to be in my arms just as much as I long to hold him? The doctors tell me no; they say he has virtually no brain activity, but how can anyone know for sure?

The doctors told us today that not just his brain, but his heart and kidneys are failing too. It's really just the machines keeping him alive now. We don't have much time. Sitting here in the NICU and seeing that all the other babies around us are crying and kicking and breathing hurts terribly. Even though they are sick, they will most likely eventually go home. Our Landon will never cry, open his eyes, wiggle his little fingers and toes or even take a breath on his own.

JULY 12

Well it looks like miracles do exist after all. Last night we took Landon off life support. The doctors told us that, at best, we would have a few seconds, maybe minutes with him. We got a whole seventeen hours. It could have been the worst nightmare of our lives, but in some amazing way—which others might not be able to understand unless they'd been there themselves—it was actually one of the most beautiful times I've ever experienced. With the help of the wonderful staff here at the hospital, we were able to spend that last night and day of his life with Landon. We were assured that with no brain activity he would feel no pain. The rest of his body was quickly fading, but it would take some time for it to stop functioning completely.

We got to bring him to our bedroom and spend the whole night with him, as if he were home with us. We cuddled and kissed every part of him. We decided his feet and ears and lips were like his daddy's and his nose and cheeks and hair were like mine. We told him about all the fun things we did when he was in my belly, and what we had hoped to do if we'd been able to bring him home. We told him about Cody and how we wished with all our hearts that they could meet. We talked about what we were going to do over the next few months to grieve and stay busy. We laughed, we cried, we kissed and we took a ton of photos. We ate soup my mom had made, and I pumped an abundance of milk, seeing that I'm a fountain now and have decided to donate my breast milk to a baby in need.

Before this week, neither of us had ever witnessed death, which is usually hidden and feared in our society. But Landon taught us not to be afraid of death, to look right at it and recognize that this is a necessary part of life. That's something people may search for their whole lives and never find. So in a way our son was our little miracle, our spirit guide. I think that he will continue to teach us great things.

During the seventeen miraculous hours without life support that Landon spent with us, we never knew if his next breath would be his last. In fact, a number of times when his breathing stopped and his colour changed, we felt sure that he was gone, but then the little guy would start breathing again. Each time, his pudgy hands would squeeze my fingers, not deliberately, but as a result of the stiffening of muscles that occurs just before death. It was hard to see at first, but once we understood that he wasn't suffering at all but simply preparing his little body for the eventual transition, we were able to relax and really cherish each moment we had with him. By the time the next morning came around and he was still with us, we were able to even find humour in the situation—we joked that he was being a little trickster like his dad, making us all believe he was gone and then, "Just kidding!"

And, of course, even though those hours of waiting were precious and miraculous, they were also agonizing. Watching him struggle to breathe, knowing that there was nothing we could do to save him, left me feeling completely powerless. For the nine months he was inside me, I had focused so completely on protecting him and keeping him safe, and now there was nothing more I could do but hold him, and wait.

I am so grateful that Landon chose to show us that yes, he was there—at least in some small way. During the minutes, then hours, that followed after he was taken off life support, he waited patiently for the perfect time to leave. He gave Justin and me a whole night to cuddle and kiss him. He gave us a whole morning to marvel at his precious body and take plenty of photos with the backdrop of sunshine streaming through the windows. He even stuck around long enough for his grandparents and aunts and uncles to be able to meet him and cuddle him.

By the time my sister, who is a NICU nurse and very passionate about the importance of skin-to-skin contact, insisted that we un-swaddle him and lay his little naked body on my chest, I was ready to let him go. I didn't want him to be trapped in a body that no longer functioned. I wasn't afraid anymore. The moment his skin touched mine, I could feel him completely relax. "Let go," I told him. "It's okay." His soft breathing slowed and soon stopped. His strong heartbeat faded away. At that moment I knew he was at peace, that he was ready to go. It was the most beautiful thing in the world.

My mom took a photo the moment Landon was placed on my bare chest, which was also the instant he took his last breath. It's strange to see that I was smiling. How did I manage to smile at the same moment that my son slipped away from this world? Thinking back, I remember feeling a deep sense of relief and imagining that he felt as though he were back in my womb again, safe and protected—at least that's what I hoped.

One of the things that has caused me tremendous anxiety over these past few days at the hospital is the thought of going home and seeing an empty car seat, the room we'd so eagerly prepared, all the gifts our friends and family had so generously given us. It all seems so cruel and unfair. How can we ever go back?

I'm starting to get used to this hospital cocoon. Inside these walls I'm able to pretend, on some level, that this isn't real life, that soon I will wake up from this nightmare. Early this morning I was able to let go of some of that fear. As the sun rose and Justin and Landon lay in bed still asleep, I tidied up the room and photographed all the things that would remind us of our stay there. I think I photographed everything three or four times: flowers, door signs, pumping supplies, blankets, the cute outfits I'd brought for him—literally everything. I found that tremendously therapeutic. Maybe it helped convince me that yes, this is really happening. This is real. And as horrible and terrifying as everything is, these four walls contain all of the memories we'll ever have of Landon's brief life, and I don't want to miss a thing.

going home without landon

JULY 13

Coming home has been hard as hell, but not as bad as I'd imagined. Our dog was very happy to see us, so at least we had that comfort when we walked into our house. Cody has a very independent personality and rarely seeks attention. But now whenever I'm crying he tries to get me to pet him, staying close and nudging my hand with his paw or nose. It's as though he's saying, *Mom, it's okay, you've still got me, remember?*

It makes my heart ache seeing Landon's empty room. I sat in his rocking chair and cried for hours this morning. The hardest part was putting away his tiny outfits that we'd brought to the hospital. I had packed a few of my favourites because I couldn't decide which would suit him best. Looking at those outfits used to bring me joy and excitement. Now they make my heart heavy with hurt. I wish I had dressed him in one of them; then at least I'd be able to remember what that felt like. But I didn't; his body was fragile and I was so afraid of hurting him.

And after he died, we could have stayed with him longer. We could have given him his bath and dressed him in the outfit he would wear to the funeral home. I feel guilty we didn't, but I just couldn't stay any longer. I was too exhausted, physically and emotionally. I had barely slept in four days. My sister stayed with him though, and she bathed him and dressed him. It makes me feel a bit better knowing that he was with family then and that I didn't completely abandon him. But I still can't help feeling as though I let him down, as though I've failed at being the mother I was supposed to be.

But Landon's room holds happy memories too. We spent so much time preparing this special place for his arrival: from the light green walls to the little windowsill garden, to the shelves filled with far more onesies, blankets, books and toys than he'd likely ever have needed. There was also all the time I spent doing yoga in there during the months leading up to his birth and sleeping on his comfy rocker-recliner when I couldn't get settled anywhere else. Justin and I have decided to leave his room as it is, but someday I think I'll add my painting table and start painting again.

JULY 14

This morning was a morning of many firsts. I washed and dried my hair, then put on real clothes and even some makeup. I went outside for the first time in a week—a week that feels like an entire lifetime.

Remember when I predicted that when my lilies were in full bloom, my baby boy would be here? Well, those lilies are all blooming. It seems strange that they can be that beautiful, that alive, while Landon is dead—probably on his way to the crematorium at this moment. But seeing them helps me feel that Landon really is here, just in a vastly different way than I ever imagined.

JULY 16

My friend Trinette visited this morning, as she's been doing most mornings since Landon died. We've been friends since six years ago, when we met training for triathlons. Since then, Trinette and her dog, Hinga, have been Cody's and my outdoor adventure buddies—running, hiking, swimming, cross-country skiing, skijoring, cycling and going on road trips to remote beaches—there's really nothing they don't enthusiastically join in on!

Other friends have visited to offer their condolences, but it's Trinette's steady presence since the day we came home from the hospital that's been making a world of difference for me. Justin and I are grieving together, yes, but we also grieve very differently. Whereas I like to talk through everything that has happened, over and over and over again, Justin prefers not to. His perspective is that since he can't fix or change what has happened, he'd rather not continue to talk about all the "what ifs" and rehash those tumultuous days. For me, talking is helpful, even though I know there is nothing that can change our reality. Talking helps me process these intense emotions that at times seem like they are about to explode out of me. Trinette listens; she *really* listens. She doesn't offer advice or reassurances. *She just listens*. That is really the most precious gift anyone could offer.

This morning Trinette made me a delicious fruit platter because she knows how much I love fruit (mangos and berries are my favourite). Waking up was excruciating because my pain medications had worn off and I was drenched in breast milk, but this made getting out of bed a bit easier.

After we'd eaten, we took our dogs to the nearby school field to play fetch. Well, at least Hinga likes to play fetch. Cody has never been interested in fetching, but loves to chase Hinga and try to steal the ball from her. The sun was shining bright and the temperature was already warming up, so it didn't take long for them to get tired out. The dogs decided to relax in the cool shade under the play structure, and soon a group of small children crowded around, wanting to pet them. "Puppies! Puppies!" they shrieked with glee. This was the first time I'd seen children since losing Landon. I watched at a distance while my heart broke a little more. This would have been Landon in a couple years—we'd often talked about how we would take him to play at this park. It seems that no matter where I go, no matter what I do, there are always reminders of Landon and everything we lost. I do not know how I'll ever get used to living without my son.

JULY 17

It's a weird feeling to go out in public these days. I feel numb and disconnected, as though I'm walking around in a bubble—I'm there, but not really. Things happen all around me, but I'm just watching, like a fly on the wall. Yesterday, on one of my outings, I overcame a big hurdle—the first awkward public confrontation. My mom and I went to IKEA to buy patio furniture for the back deck. I figured it would be a nice first-shopping outing and that the chances were slim on a Wednesday afternoon of running into someone I knew. We walked the whole display labyrinth, for no reason other than to get a bit of exercise. In the warehouse we got the boxes on the trolley and almost made it to the checkout when I heard a voice call "Amelia!" A petite, middle-aged woman with a bright smile approached me. "Where have you been? You aren't teaching yoga anymore?" She looked vaguely familiar—a yoga student of mine at some point, I assumed. "No," I responded. "I'm taking some time off." She then looked at my belly and exclaimed "Ooooh congratulations! When is the baby coming?" I mustered up all the strength I had and said, "He has come already, and he died."

Not exactly the most tactful response, but in that moment being polite was the least of my concerns. As the words left my mouth it felt as if the air around me thickened, became toxic. It was hard to breathe. Thankfully she didn't make a big deal about it (probably she had no idea what to say). We hugged, she wished me the best, and I got out of there as quickly as possible.

It was hard, but I survived. That's progress.

JULY 18

It's been ten days since Landon's birth. Ten days since our world was turned upside down—inside out. I often feel like I'm not really living my life anymore. It's as though I was plucked out of my world as I knew it and thrown into this new life I know nothing about. My life is now a blank slate, an empty canvas. I don't know what the next day, the next hour, or even the next minute will bring. All the little things that made me *me* have disappeared. My yoga practice, clothing line, cycling, running—all passions of mine—are no longer part of my life, at least for now. I'm still in tremendous pain and most of the time I don't even want to get out of bed.

This morning I decided I needed something new to occupy my mind, to start filling the empty space. I remembered again how much I loved painting, especially portraits. I got Justin to bring my painting table into Landon's room and I set up my supplies. That's as far as I got, but it's a step. Soon I'll make this blank white canvas come alive.

JULY 19

If you're going through hell...keep going.
—WINSTON CHURCHILL

Yesterday ended up turning into a really horrible day. I thought that the day Landon died would be the worst day of my life, but I was wrong. The abdominal pain I'd been experiencing continued to intensify, until I could barely move and was having difficulty breathing. The pain was even more intense than it was the day after my C-section. To make matters worse, emotionally I was feeling worse than ever. The state of shock I've been in is wearing off, and the reality of Landon's death is starting to sink in. This nightmare is becoming more of a reality.

In the afternoon I was in so much pain that my mom called for my doctor to come and check on me. After some poking and prodding, he said he thought I might have an infection and recommended I go to the hospital immediately.

The physical pain compounded by the raw emotional pain of going back into those four walls where Landon died brought me to a new low. It felt like a cruel joke. I had to go back to Labour and Delivery triage, where I had blood drawn and then was hooked up to an IV. I have very small, difficult-to-find veins. The nurse tried an IV on one wrist, which caused me excruciating pain. Then she tried the other— even worse pain. It felt like the needle was driven right into my wrist bone. At this point I just couldn't hold it together anymore. I was angry, *livid*. But it wasn't really the physical pain that was upsetting me the most; it was the emptiness and the complete and utter sense of aloneness I was feeling. *How was it that not once since I'd been at the hospital had anyone mentioned Landon?* Clearly, everyone knew. Yet not one person even said, "I'm sorry for your loss." My son DIED ten days ago and all I wanted was this to be acknowledged. All I wanted was to be heard. *How is it that everyone can just go about their jobs as if nothing is the matter while I'm living this horrible nightmare and my entire world is crumbling down around me?* I broke down—cried, screamed, cursed, dug a hole in Justin's hand with my nails. It was a full-on temper tantrum (I'm sure the entire hospital heard me). Finally, a nurse decided to heat up my arms and was able to find some good veins.

Later I was transported through the underground tunnels to the general hospital for x-rays and then to my room. It was dark and depressing, with ugly pink walls and decor that looked like it hadn't changed since the 1950s. They pumped me full of antibiotics through my IV all night. I was terribly cold, and even a pile of rough hospital blankets did nothing to ease my chill. Even so, I woke up every hour drenched in sweat and had to call a nurse to change my bedding. Eventually I just gave up trying to get comfortable. After all, poor Justin had to sit in a chair all night (although he did sneak into my bed a few times between nurse visits).

This morning I felt a little better. The antibiotics worked their magic and I'm not in nearly as much pain. I think I'll get to go home soon. If there's one thing that being at the hospital makes me grateful for—it's that at least *I'm not dying.*

When I packed a bag to go back to the hospital yesterday, I didn't bring much. I forgot a toothbrush, change of clothes, glasses, contact lens case—basically everything. (Thank goodness my mom brought these things for me this morning.) But one thing I did happen to throw in my bag was a book given to me by a friend almost three years ago: Wayne Dyer's interpretation of the Tao, *Change Your Thoughts, Change Your Life.* I had skimmed through a few chapters but never really got into it. This morning, as I sat in my hospital bed trying to occupy my mind, I read, highlighted, took notes, and wrote. There was so much rich insight that resonated with me at this time of overwhelming grief. One quotation in particular stood out to me:

> Change is the only constant in life. Everything you notice is in a cycle of coming and going. Everything! There are no exceptions. Know this and let your thoughts flow in the constancy of change...It is perfect. It is Divine. It is something you can totally rely upon. It brings flowers, it brings the ageing process, it brings rebirth, it brings new relationships... Return to it and experience your eternal essence here and now, in the temporary container you call your body and its dramas.

By the afternoon, a doctor came to check on me and decided I was well enough to go home. I couldn't have been happier to get out of the hospital. I desperately hope I don't have to go back there for a very, very long time. Upon arriving home, I realized that it's been exactly one week since the day Landon died. Exactly one week since we returned home from the hospital empty-handed. Last Saturday's return was filled with heartbreak and dread. Stepping into the home we had so eagerly prepared for Landon was excruciating. Today, returning home was an incredible relief. Being at the hospital was so emotionally draining and depressing—not to mention dreadfully uncomfortable. Nothing felt better than having a shower, sitting out in the sunshine on the deck, then curling up in my own cozy bed. Physically, I'm feeling so much better in comparison to yesterday's misery. It's amazing how much can change, day to day, week to week, year to year. Everything is constantly changing—*that's really the only guarantee we have*.

JULY 21

> If you look deeply at a flower, at its freshness and its beauty, you will see also that there is also compost in it, made of garbage. The gardener had the skill to transform this garbage into compost, and with this compost, he made a flower grow...Sorrow, fear, and depression are all a kind of garbage. These bits of garbage are part of real life... All you have to do is learn how to transform your garbage into flowers.
>
> —THICH NHAT HANH, *YOU ARE HERE*

I worked in my garden today for the first time since Landon's passing. Although I still can't do much in terms of physical activity, I was pleasantly surprised that stooping over to pull weeds is something I actually can do. Fortunately, everything is still alive, thanks to the good amount of rain we've been getting. It was nice to spend time nourishing life: pulling out the weeds crowding the pretty flowers so they can thrive again; tilling the soil so that the organic matter can continue to feed their growth; and watching the bees collect their juicy nectar.

I found the work therapeutic. Moving my body and digging my hands into the moist earth, growing and tending new life, literally helping to turn "garbage" into flowers makes me hopeful that one day I'll be able to transform all of the sadness and anger and fear in my life into something beautiful.

JULY 23

> Perhaps the butterfly is proof that you can go through a great deal of darkness yet become something beautiful.
>
> —UNKNOWN

Today Justin and I went to the funeral home to pick up Landon's cremated remains, an extremely heart-wrenching task. There's something about a funeral home that makes everything horribly stark and final. Our being there felt wrong, so wrong. We had just become parents, and there we were wandering aimless and bewildered through this new reality as bereaved parents. It pissed me off that they wanted to sell us a miniature baby-size urn. After all, his little body was now not even a handful of ash. I'm not sure why this made me so angry. I guess I'm afraid he'll be forgotten. I don't want him getting lost or hidden. I want his presence to be known, and I want his life to be known. He existed—*he lived*. It wasn't a long life, but it was still a meaningful one. I insisted we get a bigger, adult-size urn.

There weren't many designs that appealed to me. None of them suited Landon—likely because Landon isn't supposed to be in an urn. *He's supposed to be in my arms*. And then too, I wanted to get out of there as soon as possible. So we settled on the urn with a butterfly design, which looked at least a bit more pleasant than the others.

As hard as it was, it's nice to have Landon's urn home now. We have it resting on our bedroom dresser, but tomorrow my cousin is coming over to help us build a shelf above our bed to hold it and some of Landon's other memorabilia. Looking at it reminds me that so much beauty can come from dark places. Just as a caterpillar changes into a butterfly, suffering can lead the way to healing and new growth. But I know that this process is slow and organic; it can't be rushed. The caterpillar needs to be shielded and protected within a snug, safe cocoon until it's ready to emerge anew. Right now, I need my cocoon. I've never felt so weak and vulnerable, physically and emotionally, in my whole life. One day I'll be strong again; one day I'll be ready to emerge and fly, but right now

I need to stay enclosed in the protection of all the family, friends and even strangers in my life who wrap me up in their unconditional love.

JULY 24

This morning Justin, Cody and I decided we needed to get out of the city. We packed up our Jeep and drove about an hour south to a small lake, St. Malo. Although it was a cool, windy morning—a little too cold for swimming— we had fun playing fetch with Cody in the water, then watching him dig himself halfway down a gopher hole. Two gophers scurried out at one point, but none were harmed, thank goodness!

While we were there, Justin took a photo of me standing on the beach and looking out at the lake. When I saw this photo I was surprised by how normal I look: so healthy, peaceful, and carefree—like myself again. It's interesting how the angle of a camera can influence our perspective. It's often said that a picture is worth a thousand words—but how many of them are accurate? Can they show what's beneath the surface?

As we were leaving the beach, the weather was warming up and cars full of families with excited kids were beginning to arrive. Justin and I talked on the way home about how easily everyone else seems to have babies. Everyone else's kids just seem to pop out, healthy and thriving. We talked about how even though we try very hard to be happy for others who have living children, deep down there is a very real sense of anger and envy that's hard to suppress.

It helps me to remember that our perspective of the lives of others is limited. Who's to say how many have suffered losses like ours? Who's to say they don't face challenges of other kinds that are just as heartbreaking? We may just see the pretty picture, the happy and healthy kids. The lens through which we see the world can never capture the full view; it can never reveal the many layers below what might appear to be a perfect, polished surface.

JULY 26

The day before Landon's birth, I had posted a photo on Instagram of the Provencher Bridge. That was a bit unusual; before that I had only posted photos of yoga poses or other events in my life—never anything architectural. That picture of the bridge was the last photo I posted before my life changed forever. What had inspired me to take that photo, let alone share it, I'm not sure. But today I thought about the symbolic meaning of bridges; a bridge can symbolize a transition, a critical juncture in one's life, a journey from one life to the next, even birth or rebirth. Last night, while wandering around the city with some friends after a Fringe Festival performance, I was drawn to take a photo of that same bridge at twilight. And today, two weeks after Landon's death, I sense another kind of transition, a transition in my own grieving, particularly in dealing with feelings of guilt, anger and hopelessness.

One thing causing me so much pain was that I couldn't understand how I could have been so deeply connected with Landon throughout my pregnancy yet not have sensed something was wrong during my labour. The moments leading up to the C-section keep playing over and over in my mind. Why did my body fail me, killing my beautiful, healthy baby, when I had treated it only with kindness, trust and respect? Was I too selfish, too absorbed in my own coping and comfort, to realize he was in distress? HOW COULD I NOT HAVE KNOWN?

Landon's death shattered to pieces everything I knew and believed to be true: that things are best left to play out as nature intended and that I could trust the wisdom and natural goodness of my own body; that if I was healthy, strong and full of life, so too would my baby be; and that I would intuitively do what was right as a mother to protect my baby, at all costs. Now I feel I can't trust myself, and neither can I trust what is outside of me, namely the medical system. The doctors and nurses did all they could do, but even then they couldn't save Landon. So what was there left to depend on? What could I believe now, given that everything I once thought to be true and dependable had crumbled before my eyes?

While I can't say I've found answers, I think I've made a step in the direction of finding peace. I owe this to Trinette, who tracked down a wonderful Reiki practitioner and arranged for us to meet yesterday. I don't think words could accurately describe the experience I had in the two hours I spent with this sweet, elderly women in her sunny condominium. She seemed to know exactly what I needed—silence, touch, breath, prayers, stillness and a few right words. There were moments when my lungs would spontaneously fill with breath and then keep filling more and more, not because I was trying to breathe deeply, but because something outside my control was filling me up, opening up spaces like never before. I felt a tremendous sense of ease and peace. The pressure and fogginess that had been clouding my mind for so long seemed to clear.

In the burst of clarity that followed that Reiki session, I realized that so much of my pain and suffering was because I had expected Landon to live a long, healthy life, just as I expect that I and all of my loved ones will be blessed with long, healthy lives. Our son's sudden, unexpected death was a reality check of sorts—a confirmation that expectations are never a guarantee. I started thinking that if I could let go of that one expectation, maybe the grief wouldn't be as hard to handle. Maybe some lives aren't meant to be long but are exactly and perfectly the length they need to be. I couldn't have known something was wrong during my labour—this would only have caused more pain and wouldn't have changed our reality. Maybe Landon wasn't meant to live and there was nothing I could have done that would have changed that. Right now I can't see the big picture, and maybe I'll never understand it, but what I do know is I gain nothing by trying to control, blame or dwell on the "what ifs." I gain so much more by allowing, accepting and maybe even one day appreciating the "what is."

JULY 27

> The reality is that beginnings are often described as painful endings. So when you know that there's a constant beyond the present moment's disappointment, you can sense that 'this too shall pass' - it always has and always will...
> —WAYNE DYER, *CHANGE YOUR THOUGHTS, CHANGE YOUR MIND*

I'm still feeling a sense of clarity since my Reiki session yesterday, and it occurred to me today that all of the most painful times in my life have led me in the direction of new beautiful and wonderful times. My first heartbreak, a falling out with friends, a stressful semester, the decision to withdraw from my master's program just months before my thesis defence—all of these major life events that left me feeling helpless, depressed, lonely, angry and out of control ended up paving the way to new love and inspiration and to living a life that honours my most authentic self.

Of course, at those times I never saw the bigger picture, the master plan. I don't think that's possible for any of us when we are in the immediate grip of negative circumstances. Maybe five, ten, twenty years down the road I'll understand why Landon died. Maybe I'll never know, at least in this lifetime. But I know now that I can ask for help in finding peace with that unknowing and in holding on to the wisdom that, just like all other pain, *this too shall pass*.

AUGUST 2

> Goodbyes are only for those who love with their eyes.
> For those who love with heart and soul, there is no separation!
>
> —RUMI

It's been three weeks since our little boy took his last breath, since his heartbeat in his tiny chest pressed against mine slowly faded away. "Death," we call it, but I'm not sure if that's the right word. Death is so abrupt, final and objective. Birthing and grieving Landon has shown me that these boundaries are far more elusive. There are those who are living but not really alive and those who have died but live on more fully than ever.

Technically speaking, Landon was dead when he was pulled out of me, and remained that way—without a heartbeat, without breath—for fifteen minutes as they tried to resuscitate him. Where was he during this time? Did he want to come back? For our sake, I'm grateful that he did, even if it was for only four days. It gave us a chance to marvel at his beauty—his perfection. And for the time he was off life support, we were able to experience the simple joys of holding him in our arms, cuddling and kissing him. For a short while, we were able to imagine he was our healthy, sleepy newborn.

Now, three weeks later, it feels like thirty years have passed. Our time with Landon is starting to feel like a dream. I have to keep looking, over and over again, at the photos we took. It's hard to believe it's me in those photos. Even harder to remember is the time before he was born. I look at my maternity and yoga photos often, but I feel as though I'm peeking into someone else's life.

I'm grateful that we have so many photos of Landon's life, while he was both inside me and out, to remind me that all this actually did happen—that, yes, I have a son. And while his physical body is gone and the memories fade, sharing these photos and writing about him reassures me that his legacy will continue living forever.

One of the saddest things about losing Landon was the fact that Justin never really got to know him. I had the blessing of knowing Landon intimately for more than nine months. Inside of me, I felt every kick, wiggle and hiccup. He felt my emotions, my movements, my heartbeat.

I remember the first time I felt Landon kick. I was about sixteen weeks along, lying in bed trying to sleep. I felt a little tap, then another and another, almost like tiny bubbles or popcorn. He was always such an active little boy—I think he would have inherited his dad's high energy and natural athleticism. I woke Justin up just to tell him. He thought it was cool, but I knew it was hard for him to really connect with something so small and hidden. He just wanted to hold his son in his arms. It breaks my heart that when he finally got to hold Landon, he never got to feel him or connect to him in the same way I had been able to.

Although we grieve in different ways, one thing I love the most about Justin is how real and honest he is, no matter what. There is no pretending, no faking, no sugar-coating. He speaks truth even when it's not pretty. And when things are pretty, he shouts, sings and dances his happiness so completely that you can't help but feel more uplifted. I've never met anyone else that enthusiastically involved in life, good and bad. I think coping with Landon's death has been somewhat easier for me (if that's possible) knowing that Justin is feeling all the pain and the sadness, but also all the moments of happiness too. Even though he misses Landon just as much as I do, he is still able to be his silly self. He still hides in random places so he can jump out and scare the crap out of me. He still blasts catchy pop songs and dances around the house, trying to get me to dance too. He still brings Cody onto the bed for cuddles, kisses and belly rubs every day after work. He still manages to make me laugh. I think Landon would be proud of his dad.

AUGUST 3

I'm feeling a bit stronger these days. Usually I can make it through a day without breaking down. I smile and laugh more. I can go out and do things. I can talk about Landon without tearing up too much.

But every so often, something will trigger a wave of emotion. I feel my throat close up and my heart ache something awful, with sadness, anger, jealousy, self-pity or all of the above, I'm not sure. All I want to do is curl up in bed, away from it all. The hardest thing right now is seeing moms holding their babies, in real life but also in photos. How is it that they got so lucky, so blessed? I imagine how wonderful it would have been if, even just for a second, Landon would have opened his eyes, looked at me, and known I was there. I'd give anything just to have had that moment.

One consolation is that I know, when the time comes, I will have another baby to hold in my arms and to look at in the eyes. And I will never, ever, even for a second, take those moments for granted. So, already, I am imagining a future with the joy in it that has gone from me now—a joy that is different from that innocent one I would have experienced with Landon had he lived. Maybe—although it's hard to see at this time—I am the lucky one.

AUGUST 5

> The whole value of solitude depends upon oneself;
> it may be a sanctuary or a prison, a haven of repose

or a place of punishment, a heaven or a hell, as we
ourselves make it.

—JOHN LUBBOCK, *PEACE AND HAPPINESS*

Lately I've been getting used to spending time alone again. As an introverted personality, spending time in solitude used to be a welcome comfort—a reprieve. After losing Landon, being alone could be hard. I think because without the distraction of another human being, my mind can take over and the memories and sadness becomes all-consuming. Yet at the same time, it is these moments of aloneness—usually lying in bed at night—that spark my need to write. I often feel that if I can just organize what is cluttering my brain into coherent sentences and paragraphs, things might start to actually make sense. And in some ways they have.

Today Justin went back to work. Even though I have friends and family visiting, the house feels emptier than usual without his presence. He has this amazing way of making me see the lighter side of things.

This week, my plan is to keep busy. It's a coping mechanism, I know, but at this point I just have to do what I can to occupy my mind or I'll fall apart. And on the positive side, having more alone time means that I'll be able to get started on my painting (finally), prepare for Landon's memorial that we are having on his one-month birthday, and when all else fails—write.

AUGUST 7

I was surprised by the delivery of a gorgeous bouquet of flowers at my door today! It's truly the most beautiful arrangement of flowers I've seen—I especially love that there are lilies in it. The card reads, "We love you and thank you for your incredible strength and inspiration. Landon will forever be in our hearts. From your Instagram family." It's amazing how I only started to post photos on Instagram less than a year ago, and yet the inspiration and friendships that have come from being a part of this community is truly a lifetime's worth. When I'm feeling low, I read all of the uplifting comments and this gives me the energy and strength I need to get through the day. Since most of the flowers we received shortly after Landon's passing have since wilted away, this will be the perfect way to brighten our home for Landon's memorial tomorrow. It's just perfect timing.

AUGUST 8

Today was Landon's one-month birthday. At the memorial we had for him with family and friends, we had a barbecue and planted an apple tree in our backyard. There was a beautiful sunset, with rays of sunshine streaming out behind pillowy clouds and dancing around the treetops. I knew I wouldn't be able to keep it together long enough to speak about Landon, so my sister, Alissa, did. Words cannot describe how thankful I am to have such an incredibly strong and supportive sister.

She spent every moment she could with us at the hospital and helped us to relax and enjoy being with Landon during his final hours, and today she spoke beautifully to honour our son:

> Landon James Barnes, son, grandson and nephew. I wish more than anything in the world that I wasn't writing this for him. Though Landon wasn't with us for very long, he reminded us with his gentle presence that some infinities are bigger than others. In Landon's infinity he gave his parents and family the gift of time and physical presence. He reminded us of the importance of touch, that deep human need for contact and craving for comfort. A need that, until we have it taken away from us, we forget. By working hard to live for seventeen hours off life support, Landon gave his parents a chance to experience that touch, to let them know that they will always be parents, and no one can take that away from them. And once he had shown us that, he taught us how to let go and how to be at peace. Landon's soul was wise beyond his days.
>
> For me personally, Landon showed me the other side of the NICU, not that I ever wanted to be there or ever want to go back. He reminded me of the importance of compassion in my work and more than anything inspired me to work and care as if each child were my own, as Landon's nurses did for him.

In Landon's four short days, I am absolutely certain he was the most loved and thought-about baby in the world and still continues to be. He died cuddled back in the place where he lived most of his life, encompassed by his mom's arms and love. No one could ask for a better place to let go and he knew that.

Lewis Carroll wrote in Alice in Wonderland something that reminded me of Landon's life: "How long is forever? Sometimes just one second." Landon's tiny forever, will be forever remembered, cherished, and above all else, loved.

AUGUST 10

Ultimately, we're all just walking each other home.
—RAM DASS

Yesterday I went back to the Reiki practitioner I saw a couple weeks ago. I wanted to know why lately, every so often and sometimes for no reason at all, I get this fluttering butterfly sensation in my belly—like the feeling you get when you are really happy or excited—that feeling of real JOY. How could this be? I kept thinking. Shouldn't I be more sad? How is this even possible?

She suggested that this conflict is a battle between Ego and Spirit. Spirit knows, and has always known, that everything is perfect, everything is exactly the way it should be. Landon never left; he is still here with me. And he is helping to guide me on this journey we call life. Ego, on the other hand, filled with doubt and conditioned with societal expectations, says, *No way! Are you kidding? This is terrible. You should be suffering*.

Finding peace is letting go of that conflict. That doesn't mean ignoring the sadness that comes. It means still allowing ourselves to feel all those feelings: to scream, to cry, to be angry and sad, but all the while knowing that this is healing us and leading us to a closer connection and understanding of our Spirit and of God.

I think all of the conflict, struggle and suffering we face prepare us ultimately for our own passing, our own journey "home." While I helped Landon feel the love and comfort he needed to take those last few steps, I now feel as though he will forever be my spirit guide on this journey through the rest of my life.

AUGUST 11

Today I practiced yoga for the first time since Landon was born. It wasn't much, just twenty minutes of a few supported restorative postures. Still, it felt wonderful.

I could tell this past week especially that my body was badly missing yoga. My lower back was sore, my shoulders and neck were stiff, even my hips hurt just from walking. Even though I knew it would help me feel so much better, I couldn't find the motivation to do anything. Then, two books I ordered shortly after Landon died arrived in the mail: *Art of Attention* by Elena Brower and *Yoga for Grief Relief* by Antonio Sausys. I love how when you buy something online and then forget about it, when it arrives it's like opening a gift to yourself, from yourself. I found I finally had the inspiration I needed to start exploring my practice again.

Before Landon was born, I had practiced yoga nearly every day for at least five years. Now, after a month of rest and healing, it feels as though I have an entirely new body. It's as if I'm starting from scratch, with a clean slate. It's challenging but also it's a little exciting. I'm discovering so much more about myself and my body. I've really started to learn what it means to listen inwards and move from an intuitive place, rather than from a place of ego. It's also giving me a deeper understanding of what many of my students probably feel like when they first start out, and how to modify postures to work better for those with limited mobility and strength.

Also, I have some uplifting news. I've decided to attend a retreat at Kripalu, a renowned yoga centre in Massachusetts. It's called "Yoga to Redefine Ourselves after Loss" and is facilitated by the Antonio Sausys. I found out about it a few weeks ago when Googling "yoga and grief." As soon as I saw it I got the feeling that it's something I need to do— for myself, and maybe so I can also help others one day. I'm not sure what to expect, but it's giving me something to look forward to.

AUGUST 13

Although I frequently post on my social media accounts, ever since Landon died I try not to scroll through my feeds to see what others are posting. There are just too many friends posting about their new babies, and the emotions this brings up are too intense for me to handle right now. Each time I see another birth or pregnancy announcement, it's like a knife through my gut. But yesterday, I briefly checked my Instagram feed and saw a post by @yoga_girl (Rachel Brathen) about a twenty-one day challenge she is hosting called "The Yoga Girl Challenge" (*#yogagirlchallenge*). It was the very first post to show up, and I got the sense I was seeing it for a reason. I love how it's suitable for all kinds of yogis (or human beings for that matter). Unlike the usual Instagram yoga challenge, it doesn't involve posting photos of yourself doing yoga poses. Rather, each day there's an activity to do, such as "Meditate" or "Try Something New," or there's an idea to reflect on, like "True Forgiveness," "Be Fearless" and "Dreams." After reading the description, I immediately knew that this was something I needed to do.

Rachel was the very first person I followed on Instagram, back in the spring of 2013. Actually, she was one of the main reasons I decided to get an Instagram account. (A friend told me about how much she looks forward to Rachel's photos and inspirational writing.) I followed her account for months before I posted any photos on Instagram myself. At this time, I was struggling with making the decision to leave my university education behind, which was no longer fulfilling me, and to pursue my yoga teaching and clothing line full time. Rachel's Instagram was often the first thing I would look at in the morning or the last thing I'd look at before going to bed, and her words always seemed to be what I needed at that moment. Eventually, I started posting photos of my own yoga practice in August 2013 and realized there is a huge community of others doing the same thing.

After we lost Landon, my first impulse was to delete my account. I couldn't bear the thought of telling the thousands of people who were following me what was happening. But then I remembered how honest Rachel was about her grief after her best friend, Andrea, died and how reading these posts gave me perspective and a sense of gratitude that helped me through some very difficult days. So I decided to share… and share…and share. It turned out to be the best thing I could have done.

AUGUST 16

> I'll love you forever
> I'll like you for always
> As long as I'm living
> My baby you'll be
> — ROBERT MUNSCH, *LOVE YOU FOREVER*

I didn't know this before, but Robert Munsch actually wrote the children's classic *Love You Forever* in memory of his two stillborn babies, Sam and Gilly, who were born a year apart. Some of my earliest memories are of this book being read to me. I always thought it was silly that the mom keeps rocking and singing her boy to sleep even as he grows into a grown man. Now the story has so much more depth and meaning. It makes me cry to read it now.

My mom is an incredible storyteller and would always read to my sister, my brother and me before bed. When we got old enough to read on our own, she'd still read to us. Sometimes, when we got into a really good book, she'd read for hours until her voice went hoarse. I remember the first day in the hospital after the night Landon was born, she picked up a book and just started reading it to me. I have no idea what book it was and couldn't focus enough to really hear the words, but I think it offered some distraction as the morphine wore off and the reality that I was losing my son was starting to sink in.

Whenever I fall deep into sadness, I try to remember these little things to be grateful for. So many kids don't even have access to books and education, let alone a mom to read to them. One of the many moms I've had the chance to connect with online, Jenny, has started a project to raise funds to build a school in her home country of Guatemala in honour of babies who have died. She lost her twins, Sophie and Lucy, at thirty-seven weeks gestation. Like Landon, they were perfect babies and there are no answers as to why they died. She is placing the names of every lost baby she comes across during her fundraising journey on a plaque in the school (Landon's name will be there). I think this is such a wonderful idea, turning her loss into something meaningful. I'm honoured Landon will be part of it.

I hope one day I'll be able to do something like this. I want Landon's short life to have a lasting impact, a legacy that will live on. Landon's legacy.

AUGUST 18

> Yoga is not a work-out, it is a work-in. And this is the point of spiritual practice; to make us teachable; to open up our hearts and focus our awareness so that we can know what we already know and be who we already are.
>
> — ROLF GATES

Today I was driving to go pick up groceries but turned one street early and ended up at Moksha Yoga Winnipeg, the studio where I teach. After a few minutes sitting in the parking lot working up the courage, I decided that I'd go in and take a class. I'm not entirely sure what I was so afraid of. I think mostly I feared running into people I know and having to answer difficult questions.

But I'm glad I did take the class. I was able to sneak in and out without anyone noticing me (or at least quick enough that nobody talked to me). Shauna, whom I did yoga teacher training with in 2010, guided a wonderful practice. Every word she spoke was exactly what I needed to hear. I remembered why I've always been drawn to the Moksha sequence. No matter how strong or weak, bendy or tight, tired or energized I feel, I get exactly what I need. It's simple and familiar, so I can move past the physical and focus more on awareness and going within. Even though I often practice other styles and mostly teach vinyasa flow classes, I'm always drawn back to Moksha. Today, it felt like coming home. When I left I felt much lighter, like a weight had been lifted from my shoulders.

It felt wonderful to be purely a student again. I've found that starting from scratch, becoming the "empty cup," has really allowed me to experience being taught. It's tamed my critical mind and forced me to really listen—both to the words and to my body. It's given me a reason to really wake up and feel and to let go of any goal other than to *simply be*.

AUGUST 19

I can't express enough how grateful I am for all the support that Justin and I have received over these past six weeks. Before Landon's birth I had entirely cleared my schedule with the anticipation of being wholly consumed with being a new mother. So I was left with nothing—nothing to look forward to, nothing to fill the void. This was especially hard after nine months of continuous excitement and anticipation. "What am I supposed to live for now?" I remember asking my sister. Sharing my writing and photos to document Landon's short life and continuing impact was the answer I found. Especially during the first few weeks after Landon's birth, it was this online community on Instagram and Facebook that gave me a reason to get out of bed each day—something to look forward to.

Last night another bereaved mom connected me to an online worldwide memorial for mothers who have lost children ("Day of Hope"). The host, Carly Marie Dudley, ended the ceremony with these words:

> There are gifts to be found in this journey. There are friendships to be made, there is beauty to be found. You just need to open your heart to be able to see these gifts. This journey of grief is entirely yours. Like the author of a book, you decide how your grief story is written. You have the power to honour your children and create a beautiful life in honour of them. Grieving and living wholeheartedly can co-exist.
>
> I leave you all with one of my favourite quotes, by Albert Einstein: "There are two ways to live. You can live as if nothing is a miracle. Or you can live as if everything is a miracle." Our babies and children are still miracles. It doesn't matter that they are gone, it doesn't matter how long they lived for or whether they took a breath or not. May we live for them.

I remember the Friday evening we took Landon off life support. I sat in the bathroom for an hour before just so I could have a quiet space to write a post updating everyone about our situation. I guess I thought that if enough people were praying for him, maybe we'd be blessed with a miracle. We didn't get the miracle we'd hoped for, but I think we did get a miracle.

AUGUST 20

Today for the *#yogagirlchallenge*, Rachel asked us: *What are your dreams?* Truth be told, I've never really been much of a goal-setter. The life I live has been more the making of a series of serendipitous events and inspirations than the making of any definite plans.

I remember being at a yoga event when I was seven months pregnant. After the yoga class, we were each supposed to write down three dreams or goals on a postcard that was then going to be mailed to us at an unknown date. Everyone sat around chatting about their ambitions, but I was having a very hard time thinking of one. "Having a baby by July 2014!!" I suddenly blurted out. We all laughed. Of course I was going to have a baby. The thought of anything otherwise never even crossed my mind. I finally ended up writing down these three goals: teach mama and baby yoga with Landon; take Landon traveling; and be a great mom to Landon. At the time I thought they all seemed highly achievable—almost too easy—and were maybe even a bit lame compared with everyone else's big dreams. It's amazing how much can change in a few short months. Those "lame" dreams are now what I cry for—yearn for. I know that when life closes doors we are supposed to keep moving forward. *But forward to what?*

This morning I was at the beach with my friend Trinette and our dogs. We started brainstorming ideas about dreams, about things we would do if nothing was holding us back. We remembered the crazy big dreams we had as kids. Whatever happened to them? When did all those things get filed under "impossible" or "impractical"? Inspired by Carly Marie Dudley, who creates and photographs sand artwork to commemorate babies who have passed away, I wrote Landon's name in the sand. The waves crashed in and immediately washed it away. Just like that. There one minute…not even a trace the next minute. I started thinking about how similarly transient Landon's story could be, how it's etched into the world of social media but will soon be buried under layers of new and more intriguing things. The online world is so temporary, so fleeting—if I were to stop posting it would be only a matter of time before my story and Landon's legacy would become washed away, obsolete.

We started talking about the idea of my writing a book. I told Trinette that although I wanted to share Landon's story, I didn't know if I could put it in book form because I wasn't really a writer. I felt my writings were fine for social media but too amateur for print. "Well, if everyone thought that then there would be no books written except by people with big egos. And that would really suck," was her immediate reply. I knew that she had a point. So we talked more about it—how a book about Landon could be written, published, printed and sold. We came up with the idea of donating a portion of the proceeds towards organizations or projects that help bereaved parents. I decided that this could be my new dream. Just because Landon couldn't live life doesn't mean I can't live it for him.

AUGUST 21

Often, I feel angry. But Landon's death was so random, sudden, and unexpected that the anger has nowhere to go. There's no person, no disease, nothing to aim my anger at; it just lingers inside of me, and sometimes I direct it at myself: my mind starts thinking of all the things I could have done in the past to deserve this. Or what I could have possibly done differently so that Landon could be here with us today. Or how I should have spent more time with him when he was hooked up to all those machines in the NICU or after he died.

Today, for the *#yogagirlchallenge*, Rachel invited us to reflect on "True Forgiveness." I was walking on the beach and noticed that I still had remnants of the same turquoise nail polish I painted on my toes shortly before Landon was born. I hadn't been able to bring myself to remove it. It makes me sad that these reminders of his life are fading quickly: my scar is fading, my belly is gone, the little angel wing stretch marks he left on my belly are barely noticeable and my breast milk is starting to dry up. I realize that I don't want to let go. I guess part of me feels that letting go and moving forward is like accepting Landon's death as okay, and then that makes me feel angry and guilty too.

But I also know that blame and regret is not going to change anything, not going to make Landon come back. It will just add negativity in my heart and in the world, and that's not the imprint I want his short life to leave. So today I have decided to try and start practicing true forgiveness. An image came to me of pebbles that lie where water meets the shore. They don't blame the waves for one day grinding them into sand; they simply allow the water to wash away the dirt and give them a smoother and more beautiful polished surface.

AUGUST 22

Today I had my six-week postnatal checkup. I knew this was going to be hard. My doctor's office is at the hospital where Landon was born and died. It's also the place where I had all my prenatal checkups. Every Friday afternoon for the five weeks leading up to Landon's birth, I'd sit in that crowded waiting room surrounded by other women, all pregnant or with newborns. I remembered how excited I used to be for each appointment. It meant I got to hear Landon's strong heartbeat and listen to all the doctors talk about how I had the "perfect" and "healthiest" pregnancy. Each appointment had meant that I was getting closer to meeting our little boy.

Today I was the only one without a baby. Next to me there was a pregnant mom and her adorable two-year-old girl with big brown eyes and ringlets. The little girl was pulling on her mom's sleeve and pointing at me and smiling. I realized she was trying to show her mom the rainbow-coloured headband I was wearing.

I smiled back. "She's so cute," I said to the mom. "What's her name?"

"Anya," she answered. Then, "Are you expecting?"

My heart skipped a beat. "No, my baby passed away" were the words that left my mouth. I saw her face drop. In an attempt to avoid the awkwardness, I smiled and asked "Do you want to see his picture?" I showed her my phone, which has Landon's photo as my background. "He's beautiful," she said. "He really looks like an angel." I wanted to talk about Landon, more than anything. I wanted to tell her all about him—how much he weighed, how cute his big feet and long toes were, and how proud I am to be his mom. But all I could do was smile and nod; anything more and I would have completely broken down into tears. It's like the words get stuck in my throat, piling up into a painful mass that I have to choke back.

Then my name was called for seeing the doctor. He asked me a bit about how I was doing physically, but mostly he wanted to know how I was doing emotionally. I could tell he was still sad about Landon's death. (During my appointments before the birth of Landon, the doctor always treated Landon like he was already a little human—he'd talk to him and ask him how he was enjoying his "jacuzzi" in my belly). It was nice to see how much he cared, but it was hard for me to hold myself together while I was there with him and while there were all those moms and babies in the waiting room. I felt like I was suffocating. I needed to get out.

Thankfully I managed to get to the car before the tears started to flow. The pain of missing Landon went through me like a sharp knife. I'll never stop missing him. But life keeps moving on. And although often it feels like I'm moving a few steps forward, then a few steps back, I know I'm moving in the right direction.

AUGUST 25

> When we meet life undefended,
> even for a moment,
> we discover that we have no enemy but fear itself.
> In surrender,
> we choose to let our hearts break a thousand times
> instead of living our life trapped in fear.
> Each time we are willing to stay open and broken,
> the hard shields of defence soften
> and expand a little bit more.
>
> — CHAMELI ARDAGH

Before Landon, I can't remember being scared of much (other than horror movies!). During my second trimester, Justin and I took birth classes, and one of the exercises was to write down our fears and discuss them. We were so sure our baby was going to be perfectly healthy that we didn't even think to write down "death." Nobody did.

My only fear was a C-section. I probably would have been terribly disappointed about needing one had Landon lived.

It took losing everything to make me realize I can't always be in control. That at some point the only way to keep going is to surrender. To be broken. To be vulnerable. To let the hard walls of perfection and determination that I had built up around me crumble and fall.

Since Landon's birth, I've felt my heart break a thousand times. It breaks with every song that reminds me of him and each time I wake up and realize that he's still gone. It breaks again and again as I look at the photos we have of his short life and desperately wish I could hold him once more. Some photos I find easier to look at and share. These are the photos we have of Landon during the time he was off life support. But other photos still scare me. These are the photos taken the first time I saw Landon, about an hour after he was born. Up until that moment the only answers to my questions were "We don't know" and "Well, he's alive." I knew by the tone in everyone's voices that he was probably not going to survive. But actually seeing him in that incubator all helpless and alone, with wires and tubes sticking out of him everywhere, was the hardest thing I'd ever experienced. The memory still haunts me.

Today for the *#yogagirlchallenge*, the challenge is to "be fearless." So I decided to post some of the very photos I wish would disappear. I think by sharing these difficult memories, I won't fear them so much anymore. I also see how much my openness and vulnerability has been encouraging others to share their struggles and stories. That is really a beautiful thing.

AUGUST 27

I finished Landon's portrait today. I set up my art supplies in Landon's room a few weeks ago but couldn't bring myself to actually start painting until last week. It was intense and emotional work, but I liked how I got to study every tiny detail of his cute face, from his little button nose to his precious lips. I felt as though I was getting to know him a bit better. In a sense, it was as if I was bringing him to life on canvas.

When I'm painting, it's frustrating that, at times, it's such slow, tedious work. I often feel as though I'm not accomplishing anything. So with Landon's portrait, I decided to take photos of my progress every couple of hours. It was reassuring to look back and see the evolution of the painting, a bit like looking back at my photos and writings from the past two months: I can see how far I've come in my own personal growth and healing, even though sometimes I feel as though I'm stuck in one sorrowful place (an interesting synchronicity—the painting took me seventeen hours to finish and it was exactly seventeen hours that we were blessed with having Landon alive in our arms once he was taken off life support). I hung the painting in our bedroom, above the shelf with Landon's urn and memorabilia. I feel that he's watching over us as we sleep.

FALL

SEPTEMBER 2

> If you choose to see everything as a miracle, then
> where you are right now is perfect. There is nowhere
> to run to; there is nothing else to do except be in
> this moment and allow what is to be.
>
> —MASTIN KIPP

It's been exactly eight weeks since that Saturday afternoon in July when I held Landon for the last time. In the beginning, just after his death, time seemed frozen. A day felt like a year. Now, I'm wondering where time has gone. Summer is over, there's a crispness in the air and the leaves are starting to change. Life feels relatively normal again but vastly different at the same time.

Last night, I held a baby for the first time since holding Landon: an adorable four-month-old named Shaya. She has these pretty, dark brown eyes and a head full of the most beautiful, thick, black ringlets. She and her mom came to visit and pick up the breast milk I had pumped. Shaya had been in a very similar situation to Landon's: she was born by emergency C-section after her heart rate dropped suddenly during labour. Doctors didn't think she'd survive the first week, but miraculously she pulled through and was able to come home six weeks later. She has brain damage and will likely be diagnosed with cerebral palsy and still needs to be fed through a tube, but she smiles, looks around, grabs for things, and holds up her head on her own—all things the doctors said she'd never do.

I thought I would feel dreadfully sad holding another baby, but when I held Shaya I felt a glimmer of happiness. It surprised me actually—not too long ago I would have felt bitter, envious, even angry, that Landon hadn't been a miracle baby like Shaya was. But I was happy to see that Shaya has such a wonderful, proud mom and that I could help by giving her my milk (Shaya is allergic to formula and her mom's milk has dried up). I realized then that I have started to see, more and more every day, the ways that Landon's little life is making a difference in the world. Even though he died, he still is a miracle, in his own way. As heartbreaking, life-shattering and terrifying as this has all been, it is still my life, my path, my journey. And as hard as it is to accept, maybe where I am is exactly where I need to be.

SEPTEMBER 4

> Life will break you. Nobody can protect you from that, and living alone won't either, for solitude will also break you with its yearning. You have to love. You have to feel. It is the reason you are here on earth. You are here to risk your heart. You are here to be swallowed up. And when it happens that you are broken, or betrayed, or left, or hurt, or death brushes near, let yourself sit by an apple tree and listen to the apples falling all around you in heaps, wasting their sweetness. Tell yourself that you tasted as many as you could.
>
> —LOUISE ERDICH, *THE PAINTED DRUM*

Today, I taught my first yoga class since Landon died. I debated whether going back to teaching was a good idea or not. While part of me was terrified of facing all my students I'd taught up until the end of my pregnancy, I also knew that teaching would probably help me get out of my own head and focus my attention on others for awhile. And, after all, going back probably wasn't going to get any easier.

I read a quote by Louise Erdich to start the class. I thought that if I read someone else's words rather than try to speak my own, I might be able to hold it together. Still, by the time I got to the end I was practically choking on the words. Somehow I managed to finish, say a few of my own words (something about being fearless), and guide them into child's pose.

Then I froze. I tried to speak but no words came out. I

panicked. For a split second I considered running for the door. Somehow I managed to pull myself together and begin to teach. It was a beautiful class, really. The powerful energy of over forty loving, breathing, moving yogis was incredible.

I remember three summers ago I was at a five-day workshop with yoga teacher Seane Corn. When asked how she stays inspired and engaged after teaching for more than twenty years, she replied that she always tries to do things that scare her, that push her beyond her comfort zone, because that is when she is truly present. Now I understand exactly what she meant; I don't think I've ever been so present in my teaching.

I feel so relieved now that I've taught that first class. It will only get easier from here, I hope. I'm grateful that I have such a supportive manager, as well as coworkers and students who really care. How lucky am I to work in a place filled with people helping people to heal and become stronger and more flexible in both body and mind? It really couldn't be more perfect.

SEPTEMBER 5

I taught another yoga class this morning. I was at the front desk signing students in, and one of my regular students, Mackenzie, arrived. She was waving her phone around in the air excitedly. "Congratulations!" she exclaimed. Seeing my bewildered face, she continued, "You won! A trip to Thailand for @yoga_girl's retreat! Haven't you heard? She gave away two spots to participants of the *#yogagirlchallenge*, and you got one of them!"

I couldn't believe it at first. Was this for real? I'd never won anything in my life, let alone something as huge as this. I remember seeing photos Rachel posted of her retreats and thinking it would be so awesome if I could someday go. But it never dawned on me that this would actually become a reality! The retreat is in February, which is perfect because that's usually the hardest month of winter for me to get through. I'm already dreading the cold, dark months ahead, but this news made it feel much more bearable. Although it's hard to feel excited about much these days, at the moment of hearing about winning the trip I was filled with joy.

SEPTEMBER 8

Today would have been Landon's two-month birthday. It's hard to imagine he would still be so little. Most moms I know talk about how the newborn phase flies by. Apparently, when you are grieving, the opposite is true. It feels like these two months have been a lifetime.

Sometimes people ask when I want to try to get pregnant again. As much as I want a baby, part of me feels that I have to "raise" Landon first. That even though he's not here, I have to keep being his mom. If I had another baby right away, I think I'd feel like I was neglecting Landon. I know it's weird, but that's just how I feel, so I'll wait awhile, until Landon is "older" and doesn't need so much attention.

I can see, though, that with each day passing some things get a bit easier. I can now sometimes talk about Landon without crying too much and may even smile when I'm telling others about him. But, of course, there still are some days that I spend each minute on the verge of tears, just trying to hold it together and get through the day. I'm trying to remember that no matter how much I'm struggling, I'm not alone in my grief. Many people also have heartbreaking stories; they just might not be as obvious as mine is now. Sorrow is what makes us human. It's what makes us compassionate. It's what makes us beautiful.

SEPTEMBER 12

> What the caterpillar calls the end of the world, the rest of the world calls a butterfly.
> —RICHARD BACH

Lately I keep having this dream where I'm screaming at the top of my lungs I WANT MY BABY BACK!! over and over like a two-year-old throwing a tantrum. As kids, we were used to hearing "No." No, you can't have chocolate for breakfast... No, you can't have that expensive toy…No, you can't stay out past curfew. At the time, we probably got very upset, but as we got older we came to understand it wasn't because our parents didn't love us. In fact, it was just the opposite—they knew that bigger, better things in life would come if not every wish and desire we had was immediately fulfilled.

As grown ups, we get used to doing whatever we damn well please. We get pretty confident we know what is good for us, as well as what will cause us suffering, and we try to make the best choices possible on what to turn to and what to avoid. But still there are times when life tells us "no": a broken relationship, a tragic accident, the death of a loved one. People we love are lost or hurt. Babies we want so much to live, die. It seems the normal thing to do in these circumstances is to scream, cry, throw a tantrum, and ask WHY? In that moment, grief seems to be all there is, and the universe, God, life—or whatever else we have placed our faith in—seems horribly cruel. But I try to remember that in the large scheme of things, this is only a glimpse of my life. Keeping Landon might have brought me an immediate joy and saved me from a life of missing my first-born son. But the truth is I don't really know in what direction the rest of my life will now go, or what gifts might come out of this loss.

Maybe we are still children thinking we know what's best. Maybe, just maybe, this "no" can be understood as an act of love. As much as I'm hurting now, it helps to remember that I don't know what my future holds. There's no telling what beautiful gifts might emerge from the depths of this dark, miserable place.

SEPTEMBER 15

Love is the cure, for your pain will keep giving birth to

more pain unless your eyes constantly exhale love
as effortlessly as your body yields its scent.

—RUMI

A few weeks ago, I decided to relaunch my clothing line,
PranaVidaStyle. I started PranaVidaStyle in the spring
of 2013, mainly because as a yoga teacher I basically
live in yoga apparel, and I wanted to wear clothing that I
absolutely love and that is ethically and locally made. I also
wanted to have a job that would allow me to be a stay-at-
home mom while earning some income. It was at this time
that Justin and I decided to start trying to get pregnant. It
was a perfect fit—I'd always been passionate about art and
design. My mom saw my creative potential when I was a
little girl and put me in sewing classes starting when I was
five years old. I learned to use a sewing machine proficiently
and was sewing my own clothes before I could even ride a
bike. At university, I studied two years of fine art, design and
art history. And as a yoga practitioner and teacher, I knew
exactly what would work the best for fit and comfort. I knew
I wouldn't have time to manufacture the clothing on top of
the promotional and design side of the business, but I was
lucky enough to find a wonderful seamstress, Alicia. It really
seemed like it was meant to be—she was the first person to
respond to my advertisement and just happened to live in my
neighbourhood, about a five-minute walk away. Justin helped
me create a website, and before long I was getting some sales,

mostly my students and friends at first, but slowly it began to grow and I started shipping all over Canada, the United States and Europe.

Although I'd been passionate about my business before Landon was born, I was hesitant at first to relaunch. I just didn't have the motivation anymore. I was feeling uninspired and wasn't sure I could take on the extra responsibility, especially since I still have days when I feel like I can barely function. But then I had an idea—what if I created a collection of leggings that is inspired by the things that remind me of Landon, or give me hope? There are so many things that I associate with Landon because of their symbolic significance or because of the way they've appeared in my life at times I most need comfort. Butterflies, lilies, peacock feathers and rainbows, for instance. I researched these symbols and discovered they are associated with personal and spiritual growth, transformation and qualities of love, compassion, wisdom and strength, and I incorporated these symbols into bold, colourful prints. All of a sudden my creative mind was in action and I was excited again about my business.

Yesterday, I hosted an outdoor yoga class and photo shoot at The Forks to celebrate the relaunch. I invited a group of about twenty women and girls to join in (friends and yoga students of mine) and outfitted them all in my new designs. My photographer friends, Niki and Lee, joined us to take photos for the website. I'm delighted that the photos turned out exactly as I'd hoped they would—authentic and fun, and portraying a diversity of shapes and sizes. My vision is to empower women and girls to take pride in their bodies and their own beauty—to stand in their power and live fearlessly despite what trauma and challenges come their way.

I was very proud of myself yesterday. Not only did the relaunch go over great—everyone was really excited about the new designs—I was able to stay positive and focused even though there was a pregnant mom and a baby at the photo shoot. Usually, this would have triggered my grief, but I felt pretty good, even happy. I think it was because I was so absorbed in the event—I was on a mission; there was no time to stop and think.

Today was a different story. A fellow yoga teacher brought her baby boy to the studio after a class I taught. He is such an adorable baby. For a moment I was able to coo over him and admire how quickly he's been growing. Then all of a sudden, I felt as though I was punched in the stomach. I hid in the bathroom and cried for twenty minutes as the sadness of missing Landon washed over me like a tidal wave. My emotions are so unpredictable these days. It seems like one moment I'm feeling good, and the next I'm a complete mess. It's like my grief is either ON or OFF; it doesn't feel like there's much of an in between.

Most of the time, it's still really hard to see babies or pregnant women. I find that I'm either jealous, angry, sad, or all of the above. I feel overwhelming envy if the mom is happy and cherishing every moment with her babe. I'll be raging angry if the mom is unhappy and taking it all for granted. And then I'm sad either way because I don't really fit in anywhere—not with those who are moms, nor with those who aren't. I'm just in a space in between—a waiting room. I can't go back but don't know how I'll go forward. It's hard to find a space for love amidst all these difficult emotions. But I know love is the only cure, the only solution to any of my pain. I just wish it wasn't so damn hard.

SEPTEMBER 18

> It is not for a mother or father to determine the time our children spend on earth, for that has been determined by their purpose. Once they have fulfilled their purpose, they are blessed with eternal life.
>
> —ANONYMOUS

At least a handful of students at each of my yoga classes will be seeing me for the first time since my pregnancy and will inevitably ask, "How's the baby?!" It will be like that for a while, seeing I must have taught hundreds if not thousands of students throughout those nine months of pregnancy. My answer is usually, "He passed away in July," and sometimes I add, "but I like to think he's doing well."

Today my friend who was working at the studio and

overheard all of this said to me later: "Wow, I'm sorry you have to do that. It must be so hard." It occurred to me then that although it is hard to keep my composure, keep smiling and answer all the questions minutes before I walk in to teach a class, it is also a blessing in some ways. I'd rather have people asking about him than pretending he never existed. And I know once people know he's dead, they won't ask about him anymore. So at least this way I get to keep telling people about him. Telling them how cute he was and how big his toes were—how he had the perfect tiny nose and lips and weighed a whole eight pounds and six ounces.

Sometimes I just get blank stares and "I'm so sorry," but often I get a story. One student, a cheery older man who drives a limousine, told me about the day in 1983 when he had to identify the body of his big brother, who had been killed in a car accident. And one woman talked about a baby she lost, and another about her son who is disabled and has been through numerous brain surgeries. And what is wonderful is that these people always seem to come to the conclusion that these great tragedies led to circumstances that brought them great joys as well, which only became evident many years later.

So when people ask, "How's the baby," I'm not so sad anymore. I want everyone to know he's doing amazing things, even though we can't see him.

SEPTEMBER 21

> Grief isn't linear as I had imagined. I hear somewhere
> that it is more of a spiral, where we have to come
> back to the same places, again and again, but each
> time we've risen a little farther out if the pit.
>
> —ANNA WHISTON-DONALDSON, *RARE BIRD*

I left Winnipeg early this morning to travel to Kripalu, Massachusetts, for the yoga retreat for grief. I wasn't able to sleep at all last night. But for some reason I'm still not tired—probably because of all the adrenaline coursing through my veins.

You see, I used to be a big believer in statistics. I thought that because only a small percentage of babies die in our privileged society, then it certainly wouldn't happen to me—and especially not when I was in such good health. I didn't have a single allergy or medical condition. I'd never even been to a hospital, except when I was born. I ate all the right foods, took all the right classes, and did all the right exercise. It had been over six years since I'd had so much as a stuffy nose! How could the perfect little being I was growing inside of me possibly die? It seemed the least likely outcome of such a joyful and relatively easy pregnancy.

Now statistics scare me. Take airplanes, for example. There is only a very small chance a plane might crash. It used to be that I was totally relaxed about flying. There was too small of a chance that something might go wrong.

I rather enjoyed being up in the air; even rough turbulence never bothered me. Today, as the plane rattled and shook as we made the descent into first Chicago, and then Albany, I was surprised by how utterly terrified I was. *Screw statistics*, I thought. *Shit happens*. And the worst part? It always happens when you least expect it.

But how can you live life expecting and planning for everything that could go wrong? Justin tends to think like this; that's just who he is. He considers every possible dangerous scenario or safety hazard and has escape plan A, B and C worked out in his mind before I even begin to consider something might be risky. He always rationalizes that if you expect something, it probably won't happen, but if it does then you'll be prepared and you can prevent it, escape, or fight back. That's just what makes sense to him. I always had a hard time understanding this mindset. I tended to think that if something was meant to happen, it was going to happen, so why bother dwelling on all the "what ifs"? Now I have no idea what I think or what I believe. *Maybe I could have done something to prevent Landon's death if I had been more prepared or had expected that something would go wrong.* I keep coming back to this thought again and again. At times I feel assured that there was nothing I could have done—nothing anyone could have done—to save him. Then other times, I feel full of rage. *Why didn't I notice something was wrong?* I don't remember his movement before or during my labour—shouldn't that have alerted me? I worry that he was struggling inside of me, that he was suffering. *How is it possible that nobody noticed earlier?*

Thoughts like these keep coming back, every time I think I've let them go.

I am thankful though that I had a good book to keep my mind occupied on my flights. A student gave me *Rare Bird*, by Anna Whiston-Donaldson, at the last class I taught before I left. She explained in a note that she is a mother of two adopted teenage sons because she couldn't bear children of her own. She also wrote, "Amelia, I am a believer in guidance by Spirit. This guidance comes through nature, people and books. This book found me yesterday, and while I have not yet read it, I believe it was meant to be given to you."

She couldn't have been more right. Anna's thoughts, feelings, heartbreak and healing align with mine in such a close way. As a blogger, she also found solace in sharing her grief on social media after her twelve-year-old boy, Jack, drowned in a river in 2011. Her story is heart wrenching and tragic but hopeful and, at times, funny too. Reading stories of others who have survived tremendous loss is comforting these days; they give me hope that things will get better, even when it doesn't seem that way.

At some point after losing Landon, I figured if I could just hold it together in the early days when the pain was still raw, over time the open wound of my grief would heal— like the incision from my C-section has. But no, healing on an emotional level isn't that straightforward. There is no guarantee that today will be a bit easier than yesterday or that tomorrow my heart won't split right open again. As soon as I've dealt with or let go of one emotion that's been tearing away at my insides, another one seems to rear its ugly head, especially when I least expect it. It's like I'm spinning in circles, and at times it feels as though I'm spiraling out of control. But at least, as Anna's story assures me, this journey of healing is an upward spiral.

SEPTEMBER 23

> Compassion is not a relationship between the healer and the wounded. It's a relationship between equals. Only when we know our own darkness can we be present with the darkness of others. Compassion becomes real when we recognize our shared humanity.
>
> —PEMA CHÖDRÖN, *THE PLACES THAT SCARE YOU*

I'm midway through my week-long retreat at Kripalu. This retreat is the hardest work I've ever done—and the most rewarding and enlightening. The focus is not *asana* (yoga postures); rather, it's meditation, *pranayama* (breathing exercises), and somatic psychotherapy movement techniques that are specifically designed for processing the physical, emotional and spiritual symptoms of grief. I've come to realize that intellectually I can accept and understand Landon's death and see how our relationship continues through all the gifts and lessons he brings me every day, but on an emotional level, the pain and trauma are still raw.

Every day, I see that I'm making progress. Today, at the

most intense peak of our practice when we were reeling back and slamming our hands onto the ground and yelling as loud as we could, I saw Landon in my mind. For the first time since he died, I felt him near. The words that came to me were *Mommy, it's gonna be okay.* I got the sense that he's rooting for me.

The fourteen other participants are some of the most traumatized, grief-stricken and yet profoundly beautiful individuals I've ever met. I've really found comfort in the three other moms who have lost children. Although I'm by far the youngest in the group (almost everyone else is over forty years old), these days I connect better with those of the older generations. We came to the conclusion talking over dinner today that the main reason society has such a hard time supporting others compassionately through grief is that we fear, on some level, our own mortality. We all recognized that once people have processed intense loss and have come out the "other side," they have the ability to "sit" with death, in that they don't fear it anymore. We can be with others when they need it the most without trying to advise or fix them, rather by simply listening and holding space with them in their grief. Out of all of Landon's gifts, I think that insight might be the greatest one of all.

SEPTEMBER 24

One thing we grieving parents feel overwhelmed by is the idea that our children's lives were "cut short," and that their deaths were mistakes and are therefore unacceptable. Initially, that seems to be the only reasonable way of thinking; anything that suggests otherwise does not make sense to our shocked minds.

However, something I'm coming to realize during my time here at Kripalu is that our minds are woefully inadequate when it comes to processing grief, mainly because they are dualistic by nature. Our minds can't understand how a child's death can be both the most painful loss imaginable and one of life's greatest gifts: both a short life and a fulfilled life, both a terrible and untimely tragedy and an intrinsic part of the precise order of the universe. The mind is not okay with these opposites.

Yoga, however, in its direct translation from Sanskrit, means to "yoke," to join together, create union. It is the practice of bringing together and understanding the relationships of opposites by connecting deeply to our own heart and spirit, which *do* understand, honour and hold space for that which our minds can't make sense of. It's about learning to sit with that tension, that duality, and to recognize one simple truth: that everything is connected, intertwined—*one*. You and I are not islands floating in our own sea of misery; every being in existence is connected, a part of the miraculous whole. All actions, lives, and events are individual threads in the precisely interwoven tapestry of existence. We can see the pieces, but we cannot yet see the whole.

I'm starting to understand that even though Landon's

death feels painful and cruel, it was not a mistake. I don't have to like it or agree with it, but to not accept this truth is to deny the single most unarguable reality—that all lives will one day come to an end. Because a life ends suddenly and before we expect does not mean it is wrong and should be unacceptable. Landon's life is just as much a necessary and valuable part of the universe as the life of my ninety-five-year-old grandmother. After all, the Queen of the Night flower blooms only one night, as opposed to an orchid that can bloom for months. But do we say it is not a flower? That it is less beautiful? That it was a mistake that it ever existed in the first place?

SEPTEMBER 25

> Grief is the most untapped source of
> self-knowledge.
>
> —LYN PRASHANT

Another thing I've come to realize this week at the retreat is that there were many secondary losses that resulted from losing Landon. I lost my unscarred body, my trust in myself and my dream of the perfect birthing experience—things that previously I hadn't realized I was grieving. Even more than this, Landon's death affected me on a deeper level, beyond what I was able to understand until now. It occurred to me today that for much of life I never really felt good in my own skin. Media images in our society imply to us from a young age that we don't match up to an impossible ideal. Pride is often met with "get off your high horse" and "don't get full of yourself." To be critical and even downright hateful towards oneself can be the result of this conditioning. So I grew up feeling as though I was never enough. I developed an eating disorder in my teens that only got worse in my twenties, a combination of orthorexia (too-perfect eating), binging, and exercise bulimia (obsessive exercising to burn off calories from binging). Even at five-foot three and under one hundred pounds at some points in my early twenties, I still wanted to be thinner and have more defined muscles. Looking back now, I see how incredibly unbalanced I was, but at the time I didn't realize this. To me, calculating the exact calorie and nutritional content of everything that went into my mouth and working out for hours every day was just normal. When I couldn't keep up with my "perfect" diet, I'd swing to the other extreme and guilt-eat until I felt sick. I hated myself for not being able to be in control.

Being pregnant was the first time in my life that I truly loved who I was. I'd stand in front of the mirror every morning and admire my growing belly. During my pregnancy, I suddenly found that I was able to eat intuitivley and joyfully. I listened to my body's cravings and needs. I ate when I was hungry and stopped when I was full. (This healthy relationship with food that I developed during my pregnancy has continued to this day.) I didn't care anymore if I was "perfect"—having a baby growing inside me made me feel beautiful. He made me feel purposeful. He lit me up, from the inside. I remember thinking near the end of my pregnancy that this experience seemed too good to be true.

When Landon died, my sense of self-worth died with him. His death felt like a slap in the face—an "I told you so." During my time at Kripalu, I realized in a way I hadn't dared to before that Landon's death had evoked a feeling of unworthiness and caused me to question my assumption that I could "have it all." I felt, somehow, my son's death was a punishment or penance—I needed to pay for past wrongs or for having been blessed with a life that had been relatively free of intense suffering. I know these are irrational thoughts, of course, but that is what happens to the mind when we grieve—it is impossible to think clearly.

Here, in this supportive environment, things are becoming clearer. It is as if I'm scrubbing away layers of dirt—anger, resentment, guilt, fear—to encounter, with pristine clarity, what is really the purpose of all this pain. I'm starting to ask: *Who am I?* If I'm not the me I thought I was, or the me I was told I was, then *who am I?* And how am I going to embark on a new life, a better life, now that my old one has been dismantled?

As our teacher, Antonio, said today: "You have a kitchen with tiny windows and no ventilation, and it burns to the ground, are you going to rebuild the exact same kitchen? Or will you build one with plenty of big windows?"

SEPTEMBER 26

> Grief is when the veil between self and spirit is the
> thinnest.
>
> —ANTONIO SAUSYS

Today is my last day at Kripalu. The autumn colours are
glorious here in the Berkshires at this time of year, and
I've been spending much of my free time during the days
wandering around the picturesque grounds. I'm particularly
fond of sunrises and usually I make a point of getting up
early enough to see them when I'm travelling in new places.
Throughout the week, I've been so exhausted mentally and
emotionally that I've crawled into bed by 9 p.m. and slept in
so that I've had just enough time to get to the morning session.
This morning, however, I woke up early with the inexplicable
urge to get up and greet the sunrise. I walked down the hill
to the lake, where a thick fog was just beginning to lift. The
sun was persisting to break through, its light reflecting off the
cloud-like haze that blanketed the water. Ever since I was a
kid I've loved to swim, so I stripped down to my underwear
and jumped right in.

It was *cold*—that brain-freezing, take-your-breath-
away cold that numbs your body. I dove under and swam
around for a while, bearing the intensity of the sensations,
not because I'm crazy or enjoy pain but because I knew that
when I got out and slipped back into my cozy warm clothes,
I'd feel fantastic: clean, refreshed, alive! And I did.

After my swim, this analogy occurred to me: yes, life can be painful, dark, nearly unbearable at times, and when it is I have two choices. I can sit "by the edge" of the experience and wait for the pain (fog) to clear. And yes, the sun will eventually rise, as it always does and always will, just as optimism will rise, because no one can stay sad forever. It's just not possible. Then there is a second option: Instead of sitting by the edge and waiting, I can dive in, dig deep and bear all the pain, vulnerability and struggle that come with facing and really processing *all of it*—the sadness, anger, guilt and anxiety. I know the answer for me—I should dive in. It's by doing this that I can come up for air exhilarated, cleansed, inspired! The "veil" of my mind lifted.

It's becoming clearer to me that no matter how much I hurt, no matter how much I've lost, there is a part of me within that is untouched, unchanged and always at peace—my Spirit, or *atman* in yogic philosophy. And Spirit always remains connected with those who have gone from our physical world. I might not be able to see or touch Landon anymore, and the memories of our time together might fade, but my love for and connection to my son will never change, never diminish. Just as when people lose their sight, their other senses become heightened to compensate, perhaps in a similar way, when we lose or are separated from the ones we love, our souls grow bigger, more perceptive, more receptive— so that we can continue to love and feel their presence in our hearts even though they are not physically present.

Later today…

Well, it looks like today isn't my last day after all! There was a fire at Chicago airport air control station, and my flight out of Albany has been cancelled. I miss Justin and Cody like crazy but trust that there is a reason I need to be here longer.

SEPTEMBER 27

> We don't get over our grief, we change
> our relationship to it.
>
> —LYN PRASHANT

At the retreat, at least a few times a day, Antonio would ask "what's your word?" and we each would have to name what we were feeling at that moment. It was hard at first to pinpoint one word that could possibly come close to expressing the multitude of emotions I'd be feeling at any given time, but it got easier and easier to do as the week progressed.

At this moment, my word is "joyful." Yesterday, when my flight was cancelled, I booked into a hotel with another retreat participant, Jill, who is a pediatric cancer care nurse and yoga therapist in Vancouver. She had recently lost her mother and was also grieving the loss of two of her young patients. We had dinner together and talked for many hours about life, death and the afterlife. Her insights and stories of being present in the final moments of many young children throughout her career brought me some comfort. The things she heard her patients say after coming out of comas or moments before death leave me no doubt that they feel only pure love, comfort and joy during passing.

One story in particular touched me. A little girl, only three years old, was dying from cancer. She had been in and out of a coma for weeks. The last time she woke, she told her parents she wanted a party dress. "What for?" they asked. The little girl told them that she was going to a party and described who was going to be there. The people she described were her grandmother, aunt and a few other family members who had passed away (some before the girl was even born). The next day, she died, wearing her party dress. I feel more strongly than ever now that children, and even more so babies, who die are far more connected to Spirit than we as adults can truly comprehend.

Then today, when I posted about being stuck in Albany for yet another day (there is a backlog of passengers now and all the flights were full today), I got a message from Sarah, a bereaved mom who has been following me since Landon died. It turns out she lives close by, and so we decided to meet for lunch. Although I've been in contact through social media with many moms who have lost babies, Sarah is the first I've actually met in person. She also lost her first child, a baby boy, Caleb, soon after birth. I was astounded by how similar our stories are, right down to our labour experiences and emotions in the days that followed, the similar ways our husbands grieve, and even the heart-shaped necklace with a footprint engraved in it that we each wear. Every word she spoke could have been coming out of my mouth. Hearing about the way she was able to find the positive in every part of her pregnancy and birth experience, and even go back to work as a labour and delivery nurse and lactation consultant in the same hospital she lost her Caleb, really amazed me. Sarah is now fourteen weeks pregnant and is nearing the one-year anniversary of Caleb's birth. It was reassuring to see someone further along in this grief journey and have an idea of what my life might be like going forward. She helped me feel more confident that our boys knew only love—never fear, hurt or hunger—and, in a sense, lived the most blessed lives possible. She too will likely never know what happened to her baby boy but feels deep down that he fulfilled his destiny.

Up until now, having these conversations would have been impossible for me. Before the retreat, nearly every time I tried to speak about Landon in depth, tears would come cascading down my face and my throat with seize up. Now, it's easier to get my words out. I feel like I can have an actual conversation again. I started thinking about how wonderful it would be to have a yoga retreat specifically for moms like Sarah and me. Just meeting her and talking for those few hours was incredibly transformational. How incredible would it be to spend days together with other moms like us, talking about our babies and doing yoga together? It would be like a dream come true for me. I'm not sure I have the confidence to host something like this right now, but maybe some day…

SEPTEMBER 28

So guess what…I'm still stuck in Albany. I never expected when my flight was canceled on Friday that flights would keep getting canceled and I'd end up spending four nights here, but now I'm thinking it was really meant to be. Back in August when I booked my retreat at Kripalu, I wanted to stay a bit longer and explore New York because I'd never been there. However, "grief shatters and scatters the linear thinking," as Antonio says, and I found myself barely able to book a flight, let alone make any extra plans. So maybe this was the universe's way of granting my wish.

Today, once again through my postings, I had the opportunity to connect with Katie, a yoga teacher here in Albany, and her sister Kelly, both who have been following my blog. I took one of Katie's classes this morning and had lunch with her and Kelly. We talked for hours about life, death and pregnancy. Kelly has a two-year-old daughter, born premature after a terrifying three months of bed rest due to an incompetent cervix. Both sisters are no strangers to grief, as their aunt, uncle and two young cousins were killed in a plane crash two years ago. It was amazing to have these kinds of deep conversations within only minutes of meeting people who were really complete strangers up until then. Because they have been reading my writing, it was like they already knew me. That put me at ease because I didn't feel as though I needed to explain what had happened or how I was feeling. Katie invited me to stay with her until I was able to get a flight home, and we spent the evening hiking along the scenic Helderberg Escarpment in Thacher State Park. The fall colours were glorious. Before I started sharing Landon's story online, these kinds of connections would have been impossible. I'd never dream of landing in a place I'd never heard of and in only a few short days connecting in such a profound way with people I just met.

SEPTEMBER 29

> The soul's attachment to the body is like that of a fledgling, which forsakes its empty shell and flies away.
>
> —SUBRAMUNIYASWAMI

As much as Kripalu and Albany have been such a wonderful experience, I'm finding I'm starting to miss Justin, Cody, my home and family more than ever. Since Landon died, I think I have a much stronger need for my familiar surroundings and relationships.

Right now I'm reading *Signs of Life* by Natalie Taylor, a book Katie gave me. It's a memoir written by a young mom whose husband died in a tragic accident while she was pregnant with their first child. I can't help but be enthralled by the story of someone going through an "opposite" loss. She writes about how the bond with her son is strengthened because he is the strongest connection to her husband. Likewise, I feel my love for Justin grows even more than I thought possible knowing that he and I made Landon. The thought of losing him too is terrifying, and just being separated from him causes me stress.

One thing we talked about at the retreat was this conundrum in our culture where we tend to equate love with attachment. The psychological explanation is that this feeling of attachment or being "bound" to a mother or caregiver was key to our survival as infants, thus continues to influence our love life and relationships as adults. A lack of attachment is usually seen as a lack of love. It follows then that after a person dies, we often become attached to our grief because we feel that without the sadness we lose the ties that bind us to the deceased and that we are not loving them as we should.

Yoga, on the other hand, equates love with non-attachment. In many Eastern belief systems, it is imperative that the griever work through his or her grief and embark on a new life in connection with, but not tethered to, the loved one, so that both souls can be free to continue on their journeys. But how is it possible to not be attached to the ones we love when it is a core aspect of our humanity? The answer Antonio offered was the practice of "detached attachment," which is loving wholeheartedly while keeping a fierce awareness that every relationship will one day end. This way we truly appreciate every single moment, and we are no longer in denial of the reality that most of us spend our lives hiding from: all things come to an end. But, as with a baby bird emerging from its shell, perhaps endings are also beginnings.

SEPTEMBER 30

It seems that whenever I start to think I'm getting better, the universe is intent on proving otherwise. After a full day of diligently waiting at my flight gate, a mere few minutes before we were supposed to board, it was announced that the flight had been canceled. I was sent to the costumer service centre, AGAIN, and this time there was a very long line-up. I started to feel a paralyzing anxiety and anger overcome me.

Normally, this circumstance wouldn't be so difficult. Then why is it now? One thing Antonio spoke about frequently at the retreat was the way "new grief triggers old grief." Grief, by definition, is the normal response to the loss of people or things we are attached to. So my emotional reaction makes sense—I was attached to the idea of getting home today. Justin even took the day off work so he could pick me up and spend time with me. Actually, I was also attached to getting home each of the four days previous. Each time my flights were canceled, there was this build-up and anticipation leading to a disappointment. Although relatively minor losses, each new disappointment triggered a wave of grief, each time a little bit worse.

Obviously, "losing" a scheduled flight is not the same as losing my firstborn son. Nevertheless, it propels to the surface all the emotions of grief I felt after losing Landon: all the sadness, anger and anxiety that emerge when nine months of anticipation and attachment end in complete and utter disappointment. Each new loss is like being stuffed back into that unbearable and suffocating space of emotions.

After about two hours of waiting, I finally got to the front of the line. I handed my boarding pass to the agent. At this point I'd let go of all expectations. Fifteen minutes went by. There was lots of mouse clicking. Then, finally, he said "I'm going to get you home tonight."

OCTOBER 1

> Nature doesn't hurry, yet everything
> is accomplished.
>
> —LAO TZU

I'm home!! I arrived just after 1 a.m. this morning. Coming home to Justin and Cody was a wonderful feeling. I woke up this morning to Justin singing along to The Backstreet Boys—a homecoming can't get much better than that. Still, I started feeling a bit overwhelmed trying to catch up with all the things I had expected to get done over the past four days, particularly seeing I've just relaunched my business. Then I reminded myself that it helps to take time to breathe deeply and realize that not everything needs to be done in this very moment. Everything will happen as it needs to and as it's meant to.

OCTOBER 5

One of my students gave me *The Book of Awesome* by Neil

Pasricha the other day, which is based on the blog "1000 Awesome Things." Its premise is pretty simple—take time to notice all the little things that we tend to overlook and realize how awesome they are. Since coming home from the retreat and Albany, I've been having a hard time readjusting to my everyday life again, where Landon isn't the number-one topic of conversation and not everyone is so understanding and compassionate. One thing I've found helpful when I'm feeling down and really missing Landon is instead of mulling over all that is going wrong, I start making a mental list of all the little things, at that very moment, that are going right.

Today's list:

The sunlight streaming through the window into the bedroom this morning, and my staying in bed a little longer

The scent of fall in the air

The crackling of leaves underfoot as I walked Cody in the forest

The sound of the wind rustling through the poplar trees

Two feet that I can walk on

Two lungs that can take deep breaths

Justin's intuitive (mind-reading) capabilities—today his words, when I'm getting dressed: "Honey, stop judging yourself. You are beautiful"

Laughter

Long hugs

And more

OCTOBER 10

I've been considering for awhile now what I'm being called to do with this community of support that my sharing on social media has generated—this wellspring of compassion and love that has risen out of what's been the most difficult time in my life. For awhile I felt guilty and almost angry that anything good could come out of Landon's death. But then in a conversation I had the other day with my friend and yoga teacher, Liane, she asked, "What if this is really a divine plan to propel you into something much bigger than you can even imagine at this point, and that is Landon's gift to you and to the world... his legacy?"

That is when plans for Landon's Legacy Healing Retreat (the idea that first came to me while attending the retreat at Kripalu) really started to come to fruition. I decided I want to provide an opportunity for moms who have lost babies and children to come together and create a sisterhood of empowerment and healing. I want to give participants a chance to explore a variety of holistic healing practices and activities, such as yoga, meditation, journaling, nature, compassionate listening, counselling and art. Most of all, I wanted the retreat to be a safe and sacred space to speak freely and openly about our children, to share their stories and legacies and connect with them and each other in meaningful ways.

The retreat will be held June 14th to 19th at Pinewood Lodge, a beautiful lakeside resort in the Whiteshell Provincial Park (my favourite area to go hiking). I've started a fundraising campaign on GoFundMe.com, with the goal to raise enough money to make this opportunity—to heal, reconnect with self and develop healthy coping habits—accessible to those who wouldn't be able to attend otherwise. Any contributions to this fund are greatly appreciated. Together, we can make a big difference for bereaved moms who desperately need all the community and support I've been so fortunate to receive.

OCTOBER 12

It's been three months since Landon died. I was looking through our photos of him today, as I often do. There is one photo that caught my attention, bringing that dreaded lump to the back of my throat and the hollow feeling to the pit of my stomach. It was taken soon after Landon had taken his final breath while lying on my chest. I placed him down on the bed, and the nurse gave Justin her stethoscope. The photo captures the moment that Justin listened to Landon's heart take a final beat, then stop. Just like that, after all those hours of waiting and not knowing which breath would be his last, there it was. It's hard to describe in words the plethora of emotions I felt at this moment. I was relieved, in part, knowing that he wasn't struggling anymore. But watching his healthy-looking pink body turn a sickly grey colour and his shoulders stiffen up around this neck was too much to bear. I suddenly felt as though I was suffocating.

"Do you want to stay and give him his bath?" a nurse asked. Everything was spinning. I couldn't think straight.

I didn't want to see Landon like this, but I didn't want to leave him either. *How could I leave my baby?* Nothing has ever felt more cruel and unfair. I'm thankful my sister offered to stay with him to give him his bath; it made it just a little bit easier to let him go. She sent me a photo later of Landon in the outfit we gave her to dress him in—a white onesie with little soccer balls and baseballs dotted all over it. My stomach turned. He looked so different, so cold and, well—dead. *THIS WASN'T SUPPOSED HAPPEN,* my mind screamed. In all of the worse-case scenarios I imagined happening in my life, this was never one of them.

October is pregnancy and infant-loss awareness month. Thinking back, I can remember the thought of miscarriage entering my mind a few times early in my pregnancy. After all, some of my friends had had miscarriages. But I also had a strong feeling that everything was going to be okay. Once I got past thirty weeks, I didn't worry at all. I didn't know anyone who had experienced stillbirth, let alone neonatal death (although, as I've learned since, about 1 in every 160 births in North America is a stillbirth—that's one every twenty minutes). Of course I heard stories from my sister, but her NICU babies were most often those who had conditions such as diabetes or preeclampsia. I had no idea that at full term, after having such a healthy pregnancy, after preparing myself in every way and after being surrounded by excellent nurses and doctors and the support of my doula, husband and mom, something could go so terribly wrong. But it did. And we'll never know why. Sadly, as I've now come to learn, this is often the case with stillbirth and neonatal death—causes are revealed in less than 40 percent of autopsied deaths.

But would I have wanted to know the horrid possibilities? If I'd been asked this six months ago, my answer would been a resounding NO. Why would I want to be aware of such a terrible, unthinkable thing? Wouldn't that have just stressed me out and made everything worse? Knowing what I now know about love, life and death, I am grateful for this awareness, not so that I can live in fear but so that if I get pregnant again I won't take a single thing for granted. Not one day, not one moment, not one kick.

OCTOBER 18

I had so much fun teaching at the Prairie Yogi Magazine housewarming party today! Rachelle, the creator of Prairie Yogi, has recently opened a fantastic creative space in the heart of the Exchange, where fundraising karma yoga classes and special community yoga events will be hosted. Thank you to all who came out today—it was really an uplifting afternoon. I'm truly honoured and grateful to be part of such an incredibly supportive and unified community.

Afterwards, Rachelle and I talked about planning a fundraising event for the retreat I've decided to host. I'm excited to announce that on November 27th we will be hosting "Love, Light, Legacy," a night of candlelight yoga and live music by local musician Demetra Penner. All proceeds from the event will go towards the Landon's Legacy Healing Retreat scholarship fund. I'm feeling in high spirits now that this dream of mine is actually starting to manifest.

OCTOBER 20

> It's like a cloud in the sky. When the cloud is no longer in the sky, it doesn't mean the cloud has died. The cloud is continued in other forms like rain or snow or ice. So you can recognize your cloud in her new forms. If you are very fond of a beautiful cloud and if your cloud is no longer there, you should not be sad. Your beloved cloud might have become the rain, calling on you, 'darling, darling, don't you see me in my new form?' And then you will not be stuck with grief and despair. Your beloved one continues always. Meditation helps you recognize her continued presence in new forms. And our nature is the nature of no birth and no death...the nature of a cloud also. A cloud can never die. A cloud can become snow, or hail...or rain. But it is impossible for a cloud to pass from being into non-being. And that is true with your beloved one. She has not died. She is continued in many new forms. And you can look deeply and recognize herself in you and around you.
>
> —THICH NHAT HANH

This post is inspired by a blog post written by Amber Mongolia Hill (@aquarian_dawn), "Death is as Safe as Life Gets," which was in part inspired by Landon's story. (I love it when inspiration comes full circle!) She mentions how when she first started attending conscious death and dying workshops and writing about them on her blog and Instagram, she figured she would lose many followers. To her surprise, she found people more engaged and interested than ever in what she had to say. I, too, assumed that when I started posting about Landon many of my 10,000 followers at the time would unfollow. And yes, some did. But what astonished me was the thousands and thousands who joined me, witnessed my pain and walked with me in this journey. In just a few months, my following has grown to over 70,000, and many more join me everyday. But this "following" is much more than that—it has become a real community. Everyday I receive hundreds of comments and messages, not only from people reaching out to offer their support but also from those who share their own stories and connect with others going through similar situations. Many talk about Landon with their friends and loved ones, and I often hear how Landon's story has spread far and wide and is impacting those who aren't even on social media. I am eternally grateful.

I used to be afraid to think about death. Intellectually, I've always know it is the one certain thing, out of all of life's infinite possibilities. Everybody dies. But I was never able to contemplate or accept the fact that yes, I too, was going to die. I didn't want to think of the possibility of any of my family members dying—it just hurt too much. Now, I think it's important to confront our mortality if we want to live our lives fully. I've come to find that knowing we have a limited time here, and knowing that our loved ones have a limited time here, makes life that much more meaningful. This awareness now is what inspires me to live a life that aligns with my truest self and deepest desires. I'm not afraid to die anymore, either. I'm curious about what comes next. I don't know if I believe I will see Landon again, but I do believe that he isn't gone forever. Nothing can be gone forever. It's only a matter of what we are able to perceive or not perceive with our limited human senses. I like what Thich Nhat Hanh says about how our loved ones are ever-present in ourselves and all around us. We just don't recognize their new forms. Life is energy, and energy cannot die or disappear entirely—it simply changes forms. It brings me comfort to believe that Landon's life continues, through me and through all of you who read about him and are impacted by our story. I like to think that the love he would have given in his life on earth is being sprinkled around like raindrops falling from a cloud, touching places further than I can imagine. He lives—just in a very different way than I expected.

OCTOBER 26

One of the hardest things to deal with emotionally after losing a baby is envy. The other primary emotions of grief— anger, sadness, guilt, anxiety—are easier to express and process. I can yell, I can cry, I can do a reality check and relax. But envy—how do you deal with that? It's an emotion that comes with a side order of shame. And of course, you can't say anything because that would make you look and feel like a horrible person. So it stays, eating away at you from the inside, poisoning your heart and soul.

I cringe whenever I see happy moms with healthy living children, and it makes me sick to scroll through my Facebook feed where it seems as though every second post is a pregnancy or birth announcement. And I get emotional whenever a pregnant woman comes to my yoga class. I should be more grateful, I tell myself. At least I had the opportunity to carry a baby for nine months…at least I am still able to have more children…my time will come. But, whatever the rationalization, the grip of envy is powerful.

At the retreat Antonio taught that envy is healthy and normal and that we should honestly express it by saying something such as "I am happy for you, AND …" (what we feel about our own circumstances). He was adamant that we always use "and" instead of "but," acknowledging that we can feel BOTH. Our dualistic minds do not like contradictions and we will try to convince ourselves that they don't make sense and that we have to choose sides. But we don't. Our hearts don't think, rationalize or make sense. *They just feel.*

So here goes a try at that type of response—*I am happy for you, and your beautiful baby makes my heart ache with sadness and reminds me of all I'm missing… I am happy for you, and seeing you pregnant and full of life makes me feel empty and broken…I am happy for you, and I'm so fucking envious!* I guess I'm not able yet to do that graciously.

NOVEMBER 1

> If you know someone who has lost a child, and you're afraid to mention their child because you think you might make them sad by reminding them that they died—you're not reminding them. They didn't forget their child died. What you're reminding them of is that you remembered that they lived, and... that is a great gift.
>
> —ELIZABETH EDWARDS

Now that it's almost four months since Landon died, it's not very often that others talk about him. If he is mentioned, it's always prefaced by "I'm so sorry to bring it up..." Truth is, there isn't a second, a moment of the day, when I'm not thinking about Landon. He's the first thing on my mind when I wake up and the last thing on my mind when I fall asleep. It might seem we are having a normal conversation about the weather, food, a TV show, whatever—but in the back of my mind I'm still thinking about Landon.

Casual conversations are hard. Even if the other person doesn't know about Landon, still, for some reason, I feel as though we are dancing around the truth. I hate meeting new people who don't know that I am a mom—who don't know that less than four months ago I had an adorable baby boy—who don't know that I carried that baby for nine whole months and loved him more than anything in the world.

I want people to know that Landon existed. I want people to know that my life is forever changed, and nothing in the world could replace the piece of my heart that I lost that day in July. But what am I supposed to say? "Hi, nice to meet you. I have a son named Landon and he died"?

I don't expect others to understand. After all, before my experience with Landon, I had no idea how to act around a person who lost a parent, much less a child. But now I know...

Yes, talking about children who have died might make us cry.

Yes, saying their names might make our hearts swell with emotion.

Yes, remembering those last moments might remind us of how much we miss them.

But we are already crying.

Our hearts can't get any more broken.

We can't miss them any more than we already do.

We just don't want to be the only ones crying

The only ones whose hearts are breaking

The only ones remembering.

Talking about our children who have died can't make the pain worse.

There is no worse.

NOVEMBER 6

I understand that it's uncomfortable for others to bring up the topic of the death of a baby and that words seem inadequate, largely because the intensity of emotion is beyond anything words can convey. And yet, it is important to let those who are grieving know that their pain isn't forgotten, that they aren't alone, and that their baby's life matters. So what do you say?

From my experience, I believe that the most compassionate thing you can do for a grieving person is just BE THERE. Don't run away. Don't tell yourself she "needs space." Just listen. If a grieving mom wants to cry, let her cry. If she wants to yell, let her yell. One thing that I'll always remember was how Trinette came over the same day Landon died and just sat there with me the whole evening. All I wanted to do was show off photos of Landon and talk about him. I was still very much in shock, not even crying much yet. That is common in the early stages of grief. There is a sense of disbelief, a sense that "this can't possibly be happening." Talking about our babies and our feelings over and over…and over and over… can help us come to terms with our new reality, and then we process all the emotions once things really start to sink in.

But what if you can't physically be there? Can reaching out from afar, be it through the internet, a phone call or a letter make a difference? Trust me, it does. The tremendous support I've received through my Instagram and blog has often been what gets me through my most difficult times. These messages mean a great deal and are often more powerful and heartfelt than anything I could say or write. It gives me a sense of purpose to know that there are thousands of listening, compassionate people all around the world interested in hearing what I have to say. Many of my followers are suffering from the loss of a child as well, and it helps to know I'm not alone. They read my rants, write words of encouragement to lift my spirits, and share their own insights and experiences. It's this connection with others that reminds me that we are in this together. Things will get better. I can feel the love—even from far away.

NOVEMBER 8

Dear Landon,

Today you would have turned four months old. Not so much a newborn anymore, but more adorable than ever. We would have settled into more of a routine by now, but each day you would have surprised me with something new. It's getting colder now, so I would have had to bundle you up warmly when we went for our walks with Cody. You'd get to wear the cute teddy bear snowsuit your Auntie Jen gave to you.

I wish I could see what you would have been like growing up. Would you look more like me or your dad? What would your personality be like? Would you be more outgoing and high-energy like Dad, or more quiet and introspective like me? Would you have wanted to hang out with your dad playing sports and video games or read books and do yoga with me? What would your first word have been?

I bet you would have been an early walker, so naturally agile and coordinated like your dad. He would have taught you to ice skate as soon as you could stand up, I'm sure. You would probably love playing jokes and getting into trouble. You would be so smart, sometimes too smart for your own good. Your dad would have taught you five programming languages before you got to junior high, and I would want you to learn French and Spanish. We would read books every night before bed. I wonder if you would have loved mystery and adventure novels like I did or fantasy and comic books like your dad?

You and Cody would have been the best of friends. He would let you grab his ears and tail and maybe even pretend to ride him like a horse. When you were sad he would lick your tears as he does for me.

I just wanted you to know it's okay that you won't be able to do all these things. You had bigger and better plans, I suppose. We are so proud of you. You will always be our baby boy, perfect in every way.

Love, Mom

NOVEMBER 11

Remembrance Day. It was on this day last year that we found out I was pregnant with Landon. The night before, I had taught two classes and stayed late to practice. After doing a few poses I suddenly felt terribly nauseous and threw up all the berries I had just eaten. At that point I assumed there was likely something wrong with the berries. I thought (naively) that morning sickness was supposed to be in the morning. I told Justin about it when I got home and his first response was "M-m-m, don't you think you should take a pregnancy test?" I was doubtful. We'd been trying since January, and by September I'd finally come to a point where I decided to just let go of all anticipation. After all, "a watched pot never boils."

The next morning I decided to take the test. Almost immediately, clear as day, two pink lines appeared. I remember shouting at Justin, while still sitting on the toilet, "OH MY GOD I'M PREGNANT!" Since he had the day off, we spent the whole day together just talking and planning and imagining what it would be like to be parents.

Yes, a year ago Landon was just a blob of cells the size of a blueberry. He grew into an entire human being, was born, and has now been dead for four months tomorrow. It's so hard to wrap my mind around all that. It feels like a lifetime. Time moves incredibly slowly when you are pregnant—and about ten times slower than that when you have to keep on living without your child. I wish I could say I've learned to live entirely in the "now" and to really cherish every moment. After all, unhappiness lies in regrets, sadness and non-forgiveness of the past, or anxiety, fears and expectations about the future. Truth is, it's freaking hard. It's hard to imagine that I'll ever be truly happy again.

NOVEMBER 12

Dear Landon,

It's been four months since we said goodbye. It saddens me that we never really got to say "hello." I dreamed so often of you when you were inside of me. I dreamed about what you would look like and how it would feel to look into your eyes and say, "Hi Landon, I'm your mama!" I dreamed about how it would feel to hold you in my arms, and what it would be like to breastfeed you.

Now, since you died, I haven't dreamt of you once. Maybe because pregnancy made me have more vivid dreams. And back then you were so real, so close, nestled safe inside me. Now I don't know if I feel you at all. People tell me I'm a mother still, but I'm having a hard time figuring out how that works. Am I a mother to your spirit? To your memory? I like to think that we are still connected and that I am a mother to you on a deeper level beyond this physical world. But the truth is, I just don't know. There is no how-to guide, no baby books that tell the ins and outs of being a mother to a baby that you don't get to feed, diaper change and rock in your arms.

I hope more than anything that one day I will dream of you again, I will see you again. I will hold you and feel close to you again. Until then, just know I will carry you in my heart.

Love, Mom

NOVEMBER 13

Yesterday, I decided to go see a psychic for the first time. I'm not sure why, but I just got the sense that it was something I should do. After all, what is there to lose? I'm glad I did. She had many insights that really helped me to make sense of Landon's life and gave me much needed reassurance about the future.

One thing she said was that Landon wanted me to know it was not my fault—it was no one's fault—that he died. He was meant to be here for only four days, and that was all he needed to fulfill his life purpose. His life was a gift, and he wants me to start celebrating it as one.

She was very certain we would be having more children and that the first would be a girl. They would be healthy. It was also clear to her that we should not rush into having more children. The way she explained it is that Landon is going to be a spirit guide for my next child, but in order for him to do this he needs to get some rest. He's been very close to me this whole time, and still is, but he is very tired. He'll always be near, but I need to let him rest for a bit. I'll know he is resting when he is no longer at the forefront of my mind all day, every day, when the 8th to 12th of each month comes and passes without causing so much emotional stress, or even without my noticing.

The psychic also told me that I need to rest too. Right now my body, my mind and my heart are still grieving and need more time to heal before we have another child. She felt very strongly that I should take time off or scale back work and other responsibilities to heal and take care of myself. She suggested that I go on a vacation, if I could. Only after this period of rest and renewal will I conceive.

Then this morning, less than twenty-four hours later, another interesting encounter gave me even more reassurance that I will have more children. A woman who has been attending my yoga classes the past few weeks came up to me after practice and asked: "Do butterflies mean anything to you?" She then explained she is an intuitive, and when she took my class she was immediately overwhelmed by emotion. She saw a butterfly fluttering around me, and the words "spread your wings and fly" kept coming to her. She didn't know why or what it meant at the time, but later she heard about Landon and felt an intense need to tell me about it. She held back from saying anything at first because she was unsure of my beliefs and didn't want to intrude, but today she felt I had to know.

She also told me that she saw me sitting with children around me, close in age, and definitely more than two. She had a strong sense that in April something important, something big, will happen.

The last thing she said was to watch out for strange things going on with electricity, like flickering lights, as it's a common way spirits communicate. I couldn't think of any odd electricity happenings, and to be honest I was pretty skeptical. But then to my amazement, part way through the next class while teaching a sequence of warrior poses, one of the ceiling lights started flickering on and off for about twenty seconds, then went back to normal. I couldn't figure out any logical explanation—we'd just changed all the lights to brand new LED ones a month ago and no one has seen anything like that happen before.

I'm not sure what to make of this all, but what I do know

is that I feel a kind of lightness and peace I haven't felt in a very long time.

NOVEMBER 14

> Sorrow prepares you for joy. It violently sweeps everything out of your house, so that new joy can find space to enter...Whatever sorrow shakes from your heart, far better things will take their place.
>
> —RUMI

This morning my friends Trinette and Chalani decided we should go hiking at Birds Hill Park. Despite being a chilly, -18 degrees Celsius day, the sun was shining incredibly bright and there were little ice crystals attached to all the tall prairie grasses and tree branches. It looked as if fairy dust had been sprinkled over everything.

The intention of the walk, my friends informed me, was to talk about Landon. We talked about what his personality would have been like and what he would have looked like— what his favourite colour and favourite songs would be. We also talked to Landon and told him that we love him.

At some point during the hike, after taking a few detours and getting temporarily lost, we realized that the chickadees seemed to be following us. This intrigued me, as ever since Landon died I feel a sense of calm and happiness whenever I see chickadees, perhaps because they remind me of how I imagine Landon—so cute, cheeky and playful. They always bring a smile to my face, even on the darkest days.

The chickadees kept flitting around us, coming very close, even with our five dogs racing around and scaring all the other wildlife away. Trinette put out her finger, joking that maybe one would perch on it. To our surprise and delight one of the little chickadees hopped right on. Then one hopped onto my head! I took off my mitten and held out my hand, and right away it perched on my finger, staying there for a bit to chirp a little melody and groom its feathers. For the rest of our walk we were surrounded by chickadee love; the birds even followed us all the way back to the car!

Later I learned that in Native American mythology chickadees are associated with truth and knowledge and are thought to bring good luck and success. The chickadee is symbolic of higher thinking capabilities, clarity and purity of the soul, which imply a better understanding of the self as well as that of the world. It also refers to fearlessness about expressing oneself and being happy in the self.

Interestingly, I feel that the past few days have brought this great sense of inner peace and clarity. Almost as if the dense fog in my mind is beginning to clear or the clouds blocking the sun are beginning to part. I'm realizing and beginning to express with more and more certainty the purpose of Landon's life. I can see more clearly now why he could stay only a short while in his physical body. Maybe the chickadees were doing Landon's little song and dance of joy.

WINTER

NOVEMBER 17

Lately it's been cold and grey. Everything is dead and dying. There aren't any more golden leaves clinging to the trees, the grass is brown and there is no snow to brighten things up.

The seasons have always affected my mood, and this November is the hardest. I try to find the beauty in it anyway, and I do appreciate the changes in season, but I feel like the impending winter is weighing on me like a ton of bricks. My summer glow has worn off and I feel unmotivated and dreary, and I miss Landon more than ever. This was to be his first snowfall, his first Christmas. Now we have to do it all without him. It's going to be a long winter.

But at least I know that without fail, spring will eventually come. There is some comfort in that. In the same way I know that even though I'm sad right now, it is for certain that I will be happy again (as hard as that is to believe). That's the order of the universe. Nothing lasts forever.

NOVEMBER 20

> There's a fine edge to new grief—it severs nerves, disconnects reality. There's a mercy in a sharp blade. Only over time, as the edge wears, does the real ache begin.
>
> —CHRISTOPHER MOORE

I was warned it would get worse before it gets better. I guess I figured that wasn't possible. But in truth, the sharp kind of pain that makes you delusional wears away, but the ache persists. That ache is so much worse because it is nagging, throbbing, constant—at times it feels that there is no escape. There are ways to mask the pain temporarily, but it doesn't go away. And yet because it's been four months, people begin to ask, "Are you *still* grieving?" Or they say, "It's time to get on with your life." They advise that filling my arms with a new baby is the best cure. Maybe one day it will be, I don't know. But I do know that piling a load of anxiety on top of my grief now is not the cure I have in mind. One of the unfortunate side effects of your baby dying is that you know way too many ways that babies can die. It seems like every day I find out about some new disease, new labour complication, new tragedy.

"Oh but the chances of something going wrong are next to nothing," they say. Yes, that's what I was told when I was pregnant with Landon. That's what I believed. Now I know the truth. Babies do die. Every day. And sometimes for no known reason.

And then there is miscarriage. "Oh but that's just nature's way; it's totally normal and common," they say. As if that's supposed to make me feel better.

It's not just a baby and all the dreams I've lost. I lost the old me. I'm stuck in a body that won't work the way it used to, that constantly hurts in one way or another. I've lost all confidence in my body to support and protect a growing human being. For all I know my uterus is a lethal weapon. I do want a baby at some point, but right now I'm not sure I have the strength, or courage, to carry another child.

One thing I am sure of though is that true happiness is an inside job. Looking outside of ourselves for most of our fulfillment is a recipe for disappointment. I need to find my own happiness first if I want to be able to experience all of the joys of pregnancy and motherhood as much as I possibly can. I need to learn to love and care for myself again before I can expect to be able to love and care for my future children in all the ways that I dream.

NOVEMBER 25

When I got home this afternoon there was a mysterious box on my doorstep. I opened it and found an incredibly thoughtful care basket from my dear Facebook friend Tiffany and her support group, Sweet Grace Ministries. It was such a wonderful surprise! Tiffany is the creator of the Queen B Project, a non-profit that provides connections and resources for baby-loss families, as well as donates comfort bags and CuddleCots (cooling devices that allow families to spend more time with their babies after they have died) to hospitals. She gave birth to a baby girl, Emma Grace, who was stillborn at thirty-nine weeks, just ten days after I had Landon.

Earlier in the day I had been having tea with my friend, and at some point in our conversation she said "You must sometimes ask 'why me?'" I thought about that and realized I had never actually asked that question. As hard as it was, I remember thinking right from the beginning that if anyone had to be handed such a heart-shattering and life-altering loss—a mother's worst nightmare—why *not* me? Throughout my life, I've had enough food to eat and safe water to drink; I've had a warm house to live in and family and friends who will support me through hell and back. I have a wide network of friends, some of whom I've never even met in person, and sometimes even total strangers reach out and support my healing in so many ways. I have a wonderful job where I am surrounded by the most understanding and accommodating people who all want to support my healing. If anyone could go through this, it should be me.

Whenever I get overwhelmed by how hard things are, I try to remember all the women living in places where infant death is so common that nearly every woman has lost a baby, or two, or three. Or I think of all the women who don't have the resources or support I have, or of those who struggle every day to feed and protect their children, sacrificing their own health and well-being.

So yes, sometimes I get sucked into my grief and feel singled out by having my dreams and happiness robbed. It's easy to feel as though I got the short end of the stick. But at the same time I can't imagine anyone better equipped to navigate these treacherous waters, with so many lifeboats to hold me afloat.

NOVEMBER 28

Last night was the first "Love, Light, Legacy" candlelight karma yoga class at Prairie Yogi to raise funds for the retreat in June. It was such a powerful event. Reporters from the local television network heard about it and filmed a portion of the class as well as interviewed me. My first television interview was nerve-wracking but I'm glad to be spreading awareness about infant death and the retreat.

A few days before the event, I had asked my followers for the names of lost babies they would like to honour by having their names written on candle holders. In response to this post, I received over four hundred names. Although I wasn't able to use all of them (there were only thirty candles), it was apparent that baby-loss is something that affects so many. I became even more driven in my mission to spread awareness and open up conversations on this taboo topic. During the yoga class that I taught, these candles were placed at each person's mat. It warmed my heart to see that after the class, many of the participants were talking about "their" babies— admiring his or her name, and wondering how the parents and loved ones were doing.

Demetra Penner accompanied the class with her soaring, ethereal voice and keyboard that pulled heartstrings and filled the sacred space with healing vibrations. To conclude the evening, she played a cover of "Loose Ends" by Grassmarket, which meant so much to me. The song was introduced to me by a follower of my blog who lives in Halifax, Nova Scotia. Her friend, the lead singer in the band, wrote "Loose Ends" after her nephew was stillborn at forty weeks. I listened to it many times on repeat in the first few months after Landon died. The mournful melody and lyrics still make me cry every time I listen, but it's comforting to hear my thoughts and emotions so perfectly communicated through song. I know I'm not alone; there are others who understand this unbearable weight of unanswered questions and empty arms.

NOVEMBER 30

The other day I attended a traditional women's sharing circle hosted by an Ojibway woman I know. The ceremony was wonderful—we did a smudge with aromatic sage, sweet grass and cedar; we drummed and we sang. But the most beautiful thing was connecting with the other women. They were of many walks of life and all strangers to me, yet there seemed to be a common thread of yearning—a need for guidance, ceremony and connection—that brought us all there.

One woman in particular caught my interest. She was a woman who looked to be in her late thirties, with a pretty face and long, wavy, greying hair. She had a newborn baby boy at her breast and a beautiful little two-year-old girl running around. Both children had dark brown hair, black eyes and the most precious little features. The baby boy was the most content child I'd ever seen. He never cried or fussed once during the whole afternoon; he just ate and slept. His mom made mothering look as easy and natural as breathing. I couldn't help but feel an intense sense of envy creeping in.

We started the sharing circle, and each of us introduced ourselves and talked about what brought us there. I shared my story about Landon. To my surprise, the mom's turn came and she said that she had heard about my Landon. She'd happened to come across our story through the fundraising campaign I created for the retreat on GoFundMe.com but didn't know I was Landon's mom until I spoke about him. She then went on to tell about her other daughter, her living daughter's identical twin, who died suddenly at six months of age from an undiagnosed heart condition. Her baby boy is her "rainbow" baby (a baby born after a loss).

We spent the remainder of the afternoon sharing about our babies and grief. It occurred to me that if we had met in any other scenario, we most likely would never have talked about our babies. I wondered how many other grieving mothers I unknowingly cross paths with every day. Losing a child is such a silent grief, a quiet pain, one that is not noticeable from the outside, which makes it worse in a way because on the inside we are screaming, yelling, crying.

DECEMBER 14

> There is a story of a woman running away from tigers. She runs and runs and the tigers are getting closer and closer. When she comes to the edge of a cliff, she sees some vines there, so she climbs down and holds on to the vines. Looking down, she sees that there are tigers below her as well. She then notices that a mouse is gnawing away at the vine to which she is clinging. She also sees a beautiful little bunch of strawberries close to her, growing out of a clump of grass. She looks up and she looks down. She looks at the mouse. Then she just takes a strawberry, puts it in her mouth, and enjoys it thoroughly. Tigers above, tigers below. This is actually the predicament that we are always in... We could get depressed about it, or we could finally appreciate it and delight in the preciousness of every single moment of our life.
>
> —PEMA CHÖDRÖN, *THE WISDOM OF NO ESCAPE*

There are times I get this uncontrollable sense that I need to escape, to get as far away as I can, as fast as I can. This is more and more the case as I try to muddle through the obligations of this unforgiving holiday season. For one thing, I've never been a fan of small talk, never liked having to come up with words to fill the space, to be sociable and "normal." That seems oh-so pointless to me, especially now. Since losing Landon, I *hate* that obligation. But 'tis the season of Christmas parties, family gatherings, keeping up appearances. I feel like I'm being smothered under layer upon layer of lies, fake smiles and forced laughs. I find myself resenting that my suffering isn't at the forefront of everyone's mind. But the truth is—they've moved on. My sadness is my own now. How ironic it is to be surrounded by people but feel more alone than I'd ever imagine possible.

At a Christmas party the other day, where an acquaintance brought her newborn baby, I felt like I was being tortured. While watching this tiny baby be shown off and cuddled, all I could think about was Landon and how much I wanted him to be alive and with me. The worst part is that nobody talks about Landon anymore or acknowledges that he even existed. All I could think of at that party was, *How dare they be so inconsiderate? Can't people understand how much this hurts?* I knew I was being unreasonable—surely the world can't revolve around me and my emotions. I can't expect others to understand my pain. Still, the anger and envy burned me up inside. Things around me started spinning and I knew I needed to get out. Justin and I left the party early, but that didn't help. I felt even more desperate because I knew that there really is no way out, no red exit sign, no escape—this is my life now, like it or not. But I just don't have the energy to try keeping it together anymore. It's so hard moving forward when you would give anything to go back, even if just for a moment. Just to feel my son's silky soft skin again, to smell his newborn baby scent, to hear his wheezy breaths. I feel like I'm hanging on by a thread.

Maybe it's time to taste the strawberries.

DECEMBER 15

Even though things can be tremendously difficult these days, I keep being amazed by the synchronicity of events as they unfold in my life. The other day I was at the studio in between teaching classes, and it occurred to me that things seem "normal" again. I look basically the same as I did before I was pregnant, and it has been weeks since anyone has asked "How's the baby?" or said anything about Landon. And even the memories about him have started to blur—the whole time I had with him happened so fast that sometimes it seems as though it was all a crazy dream.

Just as I was thinking this, the principal from my former high school, who attends my classes often, passed me a card. She smiled and said, "You'll be surprised!" On the back of the envelope was a butterfly, stamped in silver ink. I opened it and found a card with a charcoal portrait of a woman printed on the front. I recognized it right away: it was part of a series of cards I had made as an art project ten years ago.

On the inside I had written "In the darkest hour the soul is replenished and given strength to continue and endure." It was as though I was being given a message from my younger self. I don't recall those words having much meaning at the time I wrote them. Nor did the butterfly have any particular significance. Who would have thought that a decade later they would be exactly what I needed?

DECEMBER 16

Today I visited the Whiteshell with my mom and Cody. My mom, who is a yoga teacher and Thai massage therapist, will be teaching some of the classes at the retreat. I think it will be nice to have a bereaved grandmother's perspective, and I know that her healing hands and insight will be so greatly appreciated. We took Cody for a walk down a portion of the Trans Canada Trial, which has recently been covered with a fresh blanket of white powdery snow. The sun was shining brightly and the air was crisp and refreshing. I took a deep breath and a palpable sense of calm washed over me. Being out in the wilderness, away from the noise and commotion of the city, I could feel a kind of peace and serenity that I hadn't felt in a vey long time.

After our walk, we visited Pinewood Lodge, the lakefront resort where Landon's Legacy Healing Retreat will be hosted in June. In years past, I'd often drive by Pinewood on my way to some of my favourite hikes. Every time I'd pass by, I'd see the stunning log structure nestled into the rugged wilderness alongside Dorothy Lake and think to myself, *What a beautiful place. One day I'd love to host a yoga retreat there.* The lodge itself is the epitome of rustic beauty—the vaulted ceilings, massive stone fireplace and log staircase leading up to a spacious yoga loft overlooking the lake are all a labour of love, handcrafted by the owners, Raquel and Jeff Lincoln. If nothing else, I know that just bringing the participants to this tranquil space will be incredibly transformative.

I am thrilled at how well plans for the retreat are coming together, and beyond grateful for the over $6,000 that has been raised to help bereaved mom attendees who are in financial need. I know the retreat will be a big part of my healing process, as much as it is for those attending. I also think it's fitting that the idea was conceived in September, so there will be nine months of preparation leading up to its "birth" in June. In a sense, it's like the retreat is a second baby for me. It's nice to have something to grow and nurture, now that Landon is gone, I so desperately long for something to mother. Having the retreat to focus on is giving me a sense of purpose and is often the one thing that really lifts my spirits when I'm feeling low. June still feels very far away, but more than ever now I'm looking forward to being able to connect, in person, with other moms going through this journey of grief and healing.

DECEMBER 17

We must be willing to get rid of the life we've

planned, so as to have the life that is waiting for
us. The old skin has to be shed before the new one
can come.

—JOSEPH CAMPBELL

Most mornings, Cody and I walk through a section of forest
behind a community centre near our house. It was once
burnt down in a forest fire, and all around it is old growth,
untouched by the flames, so it's sheltered from the wind and
offers a nice reprieve on cold winter days.

I remember learning when I was young about how fires
were important and necessary for the continuity of life in a
forest. A forest that had too many old, large trees prevented
sunlight from getting to the young seedlings below. The trees
getting charred by flames or burnt down into ashes are what
opens the forest to the skies and invites light in to nourish what
is left. Seeds dispersed in the inferno germinate, bringing to
life new plants and flowers that will strengthen into a mature
forest once again.

Sometimes we need to get burnt down, too. The landscape
of our hearts might look lifeless, empty and desolate for quite
a while. But that's not forever. Nothing is forever. The sunlight
pours in once again and mixes with the ashes to create the
perfect condition, fertile and bright, for regrowth, different
than before, yet formed from what was before. I guess the
question is: can I accept the death of the life I had planned so
the new one can emerge? Can I let the light in?

DECEMBER 21

> Death is not extinguishing the light, it is putting out
> the lamp because dawn has come.
> —RABINDANATH TAGORE

This weekend brought the darkest of December days: the winter solstice. A small part of me was tempted to stay in bed and wallow in misery over the darkness in my heart. But a much stronger force was pulling me towards something else. *The night is always darkest before the dawn* were the words that kept coming to my mind.

And so I found myself immersed in a weekend meditation and vinyasa yoga workshop at my friend Liane's yoga studio. Although my mind tried to convince me otherwise, something told me I needed to be there. It didn't take me long to figure out why. This is where I met Dawn. Dawn is the kind of person who radiates so much grounded presence, raw authenticity and warmth—a truly illuminated soul. I'd heard about her and the work she does as a meditation teacher and coordinator of the influential mindfulness-based, stress-reduction program at St. Boniface Hospital, but this was our first meeting.

She guided us through an opening meditation and asked each of us to look deeply at the question "Why are you here?" It occurred to me that Landon was why I was there. Although I couldn't quite understand how, I felt that he was guiding me. He knew what I needed.

She then proceeded to share what brought her there. "Mindfulness meditation saved my life," she began. In 1995 she gave birth to her second child, a baby girl who, due to a congenital defect, lived for only a few hours. She named her Ariana. Ariana has since been her spirit guide and has inspired her to become immersed in mindfulness as a career and a way of life for the past twenty years.

After the workshop, I told her about Landon and how wonderful it was to hear her story. She revealed to me that she hasn't spoken about her daughter in many, many years but suddenly felt called to talk about her at this workshop. She had the feeling that she needed to "do something for Ariana." Perfect timing (of course). I told her about the retreat, and she was immediately interested in hearing more about it. She even offered to come out to Pinewood and offer a meditation workshop for the moms attending! We arranged to meet after the holidays for coffee to talk more about our babies and plans for the retreat. It's times like these that help me remember that Landon is always by my side, bringing just the people I need into my life and guiding me exactly where I need to go.

DECEMBER 22

So much about this Christmas season is terribly difficult. Everything reminds me of last year, when we had just announced our pregnancy. Last Christmas, we were thinking of baby names and making bets on whether it would be a girl or boy. Even though he was the size of a bean, he was already part of the family. Most of our Christmas gifts were for baby or with baby in mind. I remember trying to enjoy the holiday, but mostly I was feeling terribly sick and exhausted. All I could think of was how great next Christmas would be. These days I find myself wishing I'd been able to enjoy a bit more that one we had a year ago.

DECEMBER 28

Over the holiday season I find I've been going through so many highs and lows on this roller coaster ride of grief. I decided when I was in a good place to write a letter to myself to remind me of some realizations, some truths, to draw strength from when I'm feeling low.

Dear Me,

There are no mistakes. There's nothing extra, nothing less. There are no "shouldn't haves." All the people you meet, all the events in your life, good, bad or otherwise, are unfolding as part of a perfect and unfathomably complex whole. It's like building a puzzle without the image on the box; you put the pieces together as they seem to fit but you can't see the bigger picture. You get a sense of the colours and textures but don't really know what it is you are creating. Yet you know that each piece has its place— there is never one more or one less—and ultimately it will all start to come together.

Likewise, this moment is just as fleeting as the blink of an eye, a sliver in time; but never once doubt that you are anywhere but exactly where you need to be. Even at the lowest low, so deep in despair that you believe there really is no way out, remind yourself that not for a moment is your struggle futile; not for a moment does what you are feeling or experiencing have no place. It is an intrinsic part of the whole, a necessary thread in the fabric of your existence.

Remember that the mere ability to feel the depths of your emotions is pure beauty, pure potential. To feel great sorrow is a sign that you are more than able to feel great joy. You cannot block the pain and let in all the joy. We don't get to pick and choose. It's all or nothing. After all, if you decided to toss out all the ugly pieces, how would you ever get a glimpse of the whole and beautiful picture?

Love, Amelia

JANUARY 8

It has now been six months. I remember wondering if I'd ever make it through a day, a week, and here we are. So much has changed, yet so little has changed. I wake up, go about my day just as I always have. For the most part, I do the same things, see the same people. Justin and I are parents, yes, but our lives haven't changed dramatically in the way it does for most new parents.

I think that's one thing I struggle with the most right now. In a strange, messed-up way I find myself missing that intensely raw, heart-ripped-open emotion that came in the first weeks and months following Landon's death. I think because it was so *real*. Both horrid and beautiful, but undeniably real. Time seemed to stand still. Everything around me and inside of me seemed to scream *Landon was here! He lived!* There was this brief window of time when the mundanity and routine of everyday life was stripped away. As painful and overwhelming as it was, that was time away from time. Looking back it seems even sacred.

Now it's starting to feel like it was all a figment of my imagination. I look at photos and I feel as though I'm looking in on someone else's life. Is that really us? Did we really have a baby boy? Justin likes to talk about what we would be doing with Landon if he were here, and that helps, but I'm having a harder and harder time imagining that. What would he look like now? What do six-month-old babies do?

But one thing I know is that despite life seeming almost normal, I'll never be the same. Justin will never be the same. Our hearts broke wide open, but I guess that was to make space for a lifetime of love packed into four days. *Landon didn't change our lives in the way we expected, but he did change us.*

JANUARY 15

The other day I went to the funeral for Trinette's dad, who passed away after a long bout of cancer. Trinette grew up on a small farm outside the city, and although she's lived in the city since graduating from high school, sometimes we would drive out to visit. Our dogs would play (and chase cats and cows) while we helped in the garden or went swimming in the creek. In the winter we'd go cross-country skiing at the nearby

Sandilands Provincial Forest. I didn't know her dad too well since he was often tired or in pain from treatments, but I felt as though I got to know him a little from Trinette's many stories about her life growing up. In one of the eulogies, these words caught my attention: "As soon as you are born, you are old enough to die." I know that the point was to illustrate the brevity and unpredictability of this precious life, but I found myself thinking, "No, actually, you can die before you are born."

Having a baby die in pregnancy, or during birth, is completely out of the seemingly natural or logical order of things. It doesn't fit neatly with the way we conceptualize our world; it shatters illusions of order and control. That may be why that type of death is not easy to talk about, why there is an element of the shameful or the taboo associated with it. What's more, there's an overall societal attitude that suggests, *Well, the child never really lived* or *You never got to know her, so it's not such a loss.*

When older people die, a big part of the grieving process is sharing memories of all the wonderful and funny things they did. With Landon, the only memories I have of him alive and not completely brain dead are when I was pregnant. And yet I often hold back from talking about these memories because it inevitably creates a huge amount of awkwardness. And, as much as I think I've reconciled with the fact that there is nothing I could have done differently to save him, there is still this little voice in my head that says, *Keep your mouth shut, nobody wants to hear about pregnancy from the woman whose baby died*. It feels as though, because Landon died, that whole nine months of growing and nurturing life is invalidated. And, I suppose, people assume that I must not want to talk about my pregnancy because my baby died. Yet becoming a mother is the single most important thing that has happened to me in my life. Wouldn't most people want to talk about the most important things that have ever happened in their lives?

JANUARY 16

Today a friend gave me a photo she took of a lily that caused her to think of Landon. I remember during the summer after Landon died being amazed by how, even as my world crumbled around me, my lilies kept thriving. It was as if to prove to me that in spite of everything, there are still beautiful things in this world. No amount of sadness and heartbreak can change that. As summer turned into fall, the lilies died back into the earth, and winter covered them with snow, but then they became a reminder that there is hope. Now I can't see them, but I know they are there and one day will sprout up through the dirt again, and maybe they will be even more beautiful and plentiful than last year. They remind me that life goes on even when you don't believe it will. And they remind me that everything changes but nothing is lost.

Looking at the photo brought back so many memories of when I was full of life, blooming with joy. It occurred to me that this day last year was the first time we got to see Landon on ultrasound. My doctor booked the appointment at my previous visit in December. He wanted an early ultrasound because we weren't sure of our due date. Those three weeks of waiting seemed like an eternity, and I counted down the days like a little kid waiting for Christmas.

Finally the day arrived. I remember seeing his little skeleton on the screen, perfectly formed, and his hands and feet waving around everywhere. I was completely overwhelmed with emotion. *There is an actual BABY in me!* I remember thinking. After weeks of just feeling moody and sick, I finally actually felt *pregnant.*

It was in that moment I knew what it felt like to be a mom. I would die for this little guy. Justin was even more amazed I think; his astonished expression and exclamation, "Holy crap that's our baby!" were priceless. It was all beginning to feel real. We weren't *going to be* parents, we *were* parents.

That night, I couldn't fall asleep. I lay in bed knowing that my little bean was a person now. "Hey baby, I can't wait to meet you," I told him. It was in that moment I felt a little tap in my belly—then another, and another. Soon it felt like he was doing a little dance. I don't think I've ever loved anything more than that feeling of Landon wriggling and stretching, turning and kicking inside of me, being with me every moment of the day. I was never alone. As hard as it is to live without him now, I wouldn't trade that time I had growing him, from little bud to full blossom, for anything.

JANUARY 17

Yesterday, just minutes after I posted about Landon's lilies, my cousin Jenn dropped by to give me a bird feeder that her three young boys made for Landon's apple tree. They'd filled a teacup they'd found at a thrift store with birdseed and peanut butter, and tied a ribbon to the handle so that it could hang from a branch. It was only after the boys had made it that her husband pointed out that they had chosen a teacup painted with orange lilies! I love how signs of my Landon keep showing up in the most unexpected places.

JANUARY 21

We spend so much time searching...for love, for meaning, for joy, for God

What would happen if we stopped searching, yearning and reaching out in despair and let ourselves be found?

What would happen if we stopped panicking, wandering in circles and trying to find our way and let ourselves be found?

If we sat and were still...

All we are searching for simply needs time to catch up.

All we are searching for just needs a way to get in.

FEBRUARY 4

Sometimes I just want to see his name.

There was never a doubt that our first baby boy would be named Landon. Girl names we still can't come to an agreement on, but since the beginning of our relationship nearly seven years ago (yes, we talked about having babies from the start!) we decided on Landon as a name for a boy, after the main character in Nicholas Sparks' *A Walk To Remember*. When we found out we were having a boy a year ago, our little lentil immediately became Landon. Not "the baby," not "it"—he was LANDON. And every day that passes I miss him more because he feels further and further away. It's hard to explain, but I don't just miss him as a baby, I miss him as a person—the person he was and would have become. I miss all of the things we planned on doing with him as he grew up. I miss him as LANDON. To say, "I lost my baby" doesn't even begin to convey the reality. The word "lost" doesn't even make sense—you lose your keys, you lose your wallet. Landon is not "lost." There is no chance he'll turn up in my life again, no chance I'll stumble upon him when I least expect it. He's gone forever; he's *dead.* And he is not just a baby. He is so much more—a person who would have had his own personality, interests and talents—a child who should have grown into a teenager and then an adult, who should have grown old and maybe have had children and grandchildren of his own. I was never supposed to see him die. "I lost my baby" rolls off the tongue a little easier;

it softens the blow. But the harsh reality is, *my son died*. And it hurts like hell.

People still often ask me if we want more children, and yes, we do. We're still not exactly "trying," since I'm still conflicted about whether I am emotionally ready to be pregnant again—but we're not being too careful either. After all, I'm not sure I'll ever feel completely ready. Plus, there is the fact that my period still hasn't returned since Landon was born and I feel there is little hope of us conceiving any time soon. My doctor isn't concerned (after all my period was very sporadic before and we still conceived after about eight months of trying), but each month that passes now comes with a deeper sense of disappointment and doubt. I worry, was Landon a lucky fluke? Will we have challenges conceiving? What if we're never able to conceive again? The uncertainty of it all is overwhelming.

At the same time, there's a part of me that is relieved that I'm not pregnant yet. Before Landon died I was blissfully unaware of all the things that could go wrong, and I couldn't even begin to imagine the pain of his dying. Now, the fact that babies die is a reality, my reality, and there's no guarantee it won't happen again. The worst thing that could happen is not unimaginable anymore. I wake up to live its aftermath every day.

Now I know what I'd be getting myself into. I know that to carry life means that it can also be taken away, at any time, no matter how hard I pray and how much I love. And it scares the shit out of me. But I also know that despite all the pain and suffering, I wouldn't trade the time I had with Landon for anything. And I know he would want a little brother or sister. I think I still need some time to heal, and my body probably knows this. But at this point I'm trying to trust that conceiving another child will happen exactly as it is meant to, when the time is right. Maybe there is a bigger picture, a master plan that I just can't see yet. Maybe one day this journey, and all of its setback and detours, will make complete sense.

FEBRUARY 12

I'm on my way to Thailand! Looking forward to this trip, along with writing and planning my retreat, have really been what's kept me going these past few months. I'm so excited to meet Rachel in person, and I can't wait to be able to just focus on myself, my healing and getting back into my yoga routine. As much as I've tried to keep practicing yoga after losing Landon, I've found that I just haven't had the same motivation or passion that I used to have. I hope that doing yoga daily will be what I need to reignite and rediscover my practice. I'll be spending a week at Rachel's retreat on the island Koh Samui, and then I plan to spend two weeks exploring the island of Koh Tao, where a yoga teacher I met through Instagram, Cynthia, has a yoga studio. I figured since I'm going to be flying so far, and I'm able to take the time off teaching and running my PranaVidaStyle business, then I might as well stay a few weeks. Plus, that psychic woman I saw did suggest I go on a vacation…

Yet, as much as I've been looking forward to this trip, the few days before I left I was having bad anxiety. My stomach felt like it was tying itself in knots, and I couldn't eat much without feeling sick. I barely slept. Last night, I didn't sleep at all before my alarm went off at 3 a.m. I kept double and triple checking everything, making sure I hadn't forgotten anything important. I can't help but feel like something is bound to go wrong—that winning this yoga retreat in Thailand is too good to be true. I keep waiting for everything to fall apart. I guess that's a side effect of living after your child's dies, after having all your hopes and dreams for the future ripped away when you least expect it. You have a fierce awareness that anything can happen and things don't always work out.

I'm feeling more at ease now. Justin and I had a nice breakfast this morning at the airport Stella's and said our goodbyes. I've made it to Chicago, and so far, so good! Being at the Chicago airport again reminded me of when I travelled through here in September, and I can't help but feel reassured by how far I've come since then (I'm pretty sure I spent most of that trip crying or on the verge of tears). I don't know if time heals, but I do think that time makes space for healing to happen.

FEBRUARY 15

I arrived at the retreat today! We are at a glorious oceanside yoga centre, Vikasa Yoga, on the island of Koh Samui.

I imagined this day many, many times over the past five months. Anytime things got harder than I could handle I would imagine this day: the emotion, the beauty, the love. I let that hold me up. The reality of finally being here, surrounded by an exquisite tropical paradise and connecting with such beautiful human beings in flesh, has already far exceeded all of my expectations.

I met my roommate, Crystal, shortly after arriving. She also won a spot at the retreat. We have a spectacular room, overlooking the infinity pool, lush palm trees and the ocean. Immediately I sensed that Crystal and I are meant to be here together; it's incredible how much we instantly felt a soul connection. We even look alike (so much so that everyone else at the retreat keeps mistaking us for sisters!). Her story is very different from mine, but it is also a difficult yet empowering one, of growing up in a family addicted to drugs and trying to find her way in the world through poetry and yoga.

At lunch today I sat with Rachel, her husband Dennis, and Crystal, perched atop a cliffside overlooking the turquoise sea crashing into the rocks below. Somewhere in our conversations, ranging from deeply spiritual to utterly absurd stories with elements of almost pee-your-pants hilarity, Rachel asked me: "so what are you most excited for?"

"THIS," was the first thing that came to mind. "This moment right now, exactly as it is. This is what I'm excited for."

It came as a realization later that for the first time since Landon died I'm not looking to the future; I'm not waiting; I'm not longing for some elusive destination. It feels like a dream, but I'm not dreaming. I'm not consumed by the past either. All the pieces of me that had been shattered and strewn in all directions are finding their way back. This moment, and every moment—if I just pause long enough to let it all in—is perfect and whole and full to the brim with everything and all that I need.

FEBRUARY 16

Coming to the retreat, I had no idea what to expect. I felt like I knew Rachel through our online connections, but meeting in person has been far beyond what I ever imagined. Have you ever met someone who just looks into your eyes and all your fears and inhibitions or self-consciousness melt away? Who really sees and hears *you*? That's how Rachel is. We can talk for hours, and it's like we've known each other for ages. She is so honest, grounded and present, and she radiates such powerful warmth and light. She is also an incredible listener and—get this—she learned the names of EVERY one of the forty-eight participants as we arrived and recited all of them at our welcome circle at the first class. I've been to many trainings and retreats with celebrity teachers and never before have I met someone as loving and genuinely interested in getting to know all of her students. It's no wonder she is making such a profound impact and inspiring so many people around the world. (She now has over a million followers on social media.) And did I mention she's an incredible instructor? I've been studying vinyasa for years and still learnt so much today in our classes. I'm already feeling more inspired and excited about my practice and teaching and it's only been one day! This is the beginning of something big, I can feel it.

FEBRUARY 17

Whenever I travel somewhere new, I make a point of getting up early to catch the sunrises. Even though the sun obviously rises every day back home, there's something special about witnessing this sacred time somewhere else in the world. The sunrise here is fleeting—there are a few minutes of vibrancy as the sun peeks over the horizon, then it disappears behind clouds. Its short-lived glory is what makes it that much more beautiful—it can be missed. I might look away for only a few minutes, and when I look back the colours will have become a muted glow, and then they'll disappear altogether. And there will never be another one quite like it. Landon's life was like that—only a sliver of time. But his memory is etched forever in my mind: his pudgy arms and legs and soft, soft skin; his pointy fingers and big feet; his raspy breaths and the way he'd stiffen up and clench his hands every time he'd stop breathing for a short time, until that divine moment when he rested skin-to-skin on my chest and took his last, final breath. I'm comforted knowing that even though Landon wasn't here for long, his life was beautiful. And I'm glad I didn't miss it.

FEBRUARY 18

> We think that the point is to pass the test or
> overcome the problem, but the truth is that things
> don't really get solved. They come together and
> they fall apart. Then they come together again and
> fall apart again. It's just like that. The healing comes
> from letting there be room for all of this to happen:
> room for grief, for relief, for misery, for joy.
>
> —PEMA CHÖDRÖN, *WHEN THINGS FALL APART*

Back at home, busyness had become my drug. If I could occupy my mind and body, I could keep coasting along the surface and wouldn't have to face the hard stuff. As much as this trip is beautiful and magical, it is also hard as hell. I'm finally not able to turn to working on my clothing line, to teaching yoga, to being productive and "getting things done" in order to distract myself. I have no choice but to look my demons straight in the eye, and it's terrifying.

The iron grip that grief has around my heart is slowly softening, but that ache persists. So many layers of doubt, guilt, fear, regret, anger and sadness are all rising to the surface. There is so much beauty in my surroundings, but there's a heaviness inside of me. This trip has been a series of high highs and low lows—I have profound and mind-altering glimpses of acceptance, forgiveness, love and serenity, only to have those feelings washed over with another wave of pain and self-doubt. And then I compound this with guilt over allowing myself to be consumed by the drama in my mind and not being able to enjoy the magnificence of an experience to the fullest.

"I want to feel happy. I want to feel peaceful," I said to Rachel one evening, "but it's so hard."

"Maybe you just need to allow yourself to *feel*," she said.

Just feel. Everything. The heaviness, the lightness. The anger, the joy. The jealousy, the acceptance. The guilt, the forgiveness. None exists without the other. This is my life; this is my journey. I can waste it wishing for something else or embrace all of it exactly as it is: the good, the bad and the ugly. There is never going to be a time when life matches up to all my desires and expectations; there are always going to be things weighing on my mind and my heart. I'll never stop missing Landon.

But I'm starting to realize that for all the pain, there is always an equal amount of joy. To the extent I'm broken open, there is more space to be filled with light. Nothing will ever be perfect, but maybe that is perfectly okay.

FEBRUARY 19

On the first day of the retreat, Rachel had us draw Angel Cards from a pack. Mine read "Energy Work." Quite serendipitously, one of the other participants generously offered to do Reiki on me last night. We set up a mat in the corner spot of the open-air yoga studio, or *shala*, where I practiced every day. We lit candles and arranged beautiful yellow and white flowers all around the mat.

She worked on me for almost two hours; it was one of the most unbelievably profound, mind-altering experience I've ever had. I felt as though my whole body and being was expanding and vibrating and opening in ways I never imagined possible. It was like breath was being pressed into me so that my lungs were expanding ten times beyond their normal size, and there was an electrifying energy pulsing strongly through me. I was observing all of these things happening to me as though I were watching from the outside; I had no control over my body. At one point I felt something strange in my throat and my head tilted back and I'm pretty sure I was making strange noises. By the end, I felt as though my body was being pulled into the earth, so strongly that after she was done I could barely peel myself off the ground.

By the time I pulled myself back into reality, it was late, and everyone had gone to bed. I sat out under the moonlight and stars, listening to the ocean waves and the breeze in the palm trees. I'd never felt so connected, present, calm and serene.

Today in practice we did a handstand workshop with Rachel and her husband, Dennis. I used to love handstands, and there was a point where I was pretty good at holding them away from the wall and doing fancy variations. After Landon, I just didn't have the motivation or desire to practice them anymore. I did try a few times to get back to them, but I became frustrated at having lost most of the balance and strength I used to have pre-pregnancy and C-section. I was also much more fearful. Today I finally found a lightness and strength I haven't felt since before my pregnancy. It was scary but exciting. I'm feeling like I'm slowly regaining some trust, some confidence in my body again—some trust and confidence in myself again, too.

FEBRUARY 20

I had another big breakthrough in my yoga practice today. Before Landon, backbends used to be one of my biggest strengths. I especially loved dancer's pose, *natarajasana*, as to me it is one of the most expressive and beautiful of the asanas. After Landon and my C-section, I lost so much flexibility, especially in my back, that, just before I came to Thailand, I could barely get my knee above my hips in dancer's pose. I decided to give it a try this morning and, to my surprise, my body opened right into it. I felt stronger and more flexible than ever before. I can't believe how much has changed in just one week. Partly it might be the physical effect of practicing twice a day, but I have a feeling that, even more, this transformation is very much an emotional one. My heart is opening up.

FEBRUARY 21

Today was the last day of the retreat. My heart is overflowing with gratitude. Rachel, Crystal and I said goodbye this morning—goodbye for now. I'm going to miss them so much.

Although we'll always be connected through the online world, I'm feeling blessed to have been able to get to know these women in person, beyond words, photos and videos.

After Landon died, some people would say, "Everything happens for a reason." I wanted to believe that, but the truth there is nothing on earth that could be reason enough for having to watch your precious, perfect, beautiful baby die in your arms. But one thing I do know is that my whole life—every decision, every event, every tragedy—has led me to where I am now, who I am now, and where I am headed. As much as I would give anything to be at home rocking Landon to sleep at the moment, I know that his life was meant for something more. I continue to feel as though he's guiding me in many ways, to the people I'm supposed to meet and places I'm supposed to be. One day it will all make perfect sense. Right now, I'm just trying to take it all in.

FEBRUARY 27

I have one more week in Thailand before I head back to Canada. So far I've been spending my days on Koh Tao doing yoga at Cynthia's studio, Ocean Sound, and learning to scuba dive. Each day I'm feeling so much stronger. Cynthia is an incredibly knowledgeable teacher and has helped me learn some challenging postures and transitions that I'd never had the courage or guidance to be able to do, even before Landon. Two participants from Rachel's retreat, Katrine and Marianne, have joined me here over the past couple days and we've been hiking to some of the highest peaks on the island, eating delicious Thai food, snorkeling and enjoying the beaches. As much as I'm enjoying it all, I find travelling always reminds me of how much I love home. I miss Justin and Cody terribly, and I miss my house, my friends, my family—even the snow (well, sort of!). I also really miss the crisp air and tranquil, wide open spaces of the prairies where I've lived my whole life.

In some ways I also miss Landon more now that I'm away from home. It's strange not to have his urn above the bed, his photos on the walls, and all of his things around me. I also have been meeting a lot of people who don't know about Landon, and I feel as if I'm slowly shedding the identity as "the woman whose baby died." While I am enjoying myself and healing in many ways, at the same time there's this feeling of guilt, like I'm somehow "cheating" on Landon when I'm not always thinking about him or when I avoid mentioning him in conversation.

This is a difficult road to walk—on one hand I want to embrace all the beauty and experiences here, I really do. But the more I do, the stronger I get and the happier I am, the more Landon's life fades into a distant memory. Then I find myself missing those days when he was my everything—not just when I was pregnant, but even after he died. As heart-wrenching as those days were, they felt right—as long as my whole world revolved around him and his memory, I felt like I was still a mom. I was still *Landon's mom*. Now it's harder to feel that way.

One thing that helps me is that I try to think of him as my baby who just grew up faster than most, as one who's more independent now and doesn't need all my attention anymore. But that doesn't change the fact that I'm his mom, and he's my son. It doesn't change the amount of love I have for him.

MARCH 3

> True yoga is not about the shape of your body, but the shape of your life. Yoga is not to be performed; yoga is to be lived. Yoga doesn't care about what you have been; yoga cares about the person you are becoming. Yoga is designed for a vast and profound purpose, and for it to be truly called yoga, its essence must be embodied.
>
> —AADIL PALKHIVALA, *FIRE OF LOVE*

My time in Thailand is teaching me a great deal. I've gotten stronger and much more flexible, and I've been surprised by just how resilient my body and mind are.

But the main thing I've learned about is *balance*—not just balance on my hands in a yoga pose, but balance in life. I've often tried to convince myself that at some point I will find true balance, I will find peace, I will be able to relax and enjoy life. But I've come to realize that balance is not a destination; it is never rigid or static. It is a practice of continually shifting and adjusting, playfully and without judgment. It is a practice of always coming back to centre no matter what life throws your way.

We can't find balance, but we can practice balancing. We shift a little forward, a little back, a little to this side, and a little to that. Sometimes we fall, and it's okay to fall. It's more than okay, actually, because that's when we learn the most. We just have to trust that over time and with practice we will fall a bit more softly and with a bit more grace, even elegance.

That's life—a delicate balance between holding on to what we know and pressing forward into the unknown; between falling down and getting back up; between playing it safe and pushing beyond our self-limiting ideas and beliefs; between doing what we know and find comfort in, and making possible what we thought was impossible. Balance is a process that is never ending and always evolving. So, while I may never find perfect balance, I can find peace knowing that where I am right now is exactly where I need to be.

MARCH 4

Today was my last day on the tiny island of Koh Tao. Tomorrow I begin my long journey home, which includes one ferry and four plane rides. I will miss the warm sunshine, the ocean and all the friends I've made here, but I must say I'm more than ready to be home with Justin and Cody. I miss my boys so much!

I'm also excited to get back to work, as I'm feeling full of inspiration, both for teaching yoga and with new ideas for my PranaVidaStyle business. Hopefully, springtime will arrive sooner than usual this year in Winnipeg. I feel that transitioning into a fresh season of new growth will be good for me. I get the sense that this time away has been a time of planting seeds, and coming home will be where the things I've learned can really start to take root and grow.

When I travel to the tropics, I become more grateful for the distinctive seasons we have back home. The seasons remind me that things can and do change, always. After winter always comes spring. Spring might come early or winter might drag on, but we never doubt that the earth will begin to thaw, the days will get longer and the flowers will push their way up into the light. There's some comfort in knowing that. In a world of uncertainty, it is always nice to know one thing for sure: nothing stays the same.

SPRING

MARCH 8

It's good to be home. Perfect timing too—spring might be coming early! Justin, Cody and I skated twelve kilometres on the river trail this morning, and it was beautiful, warm and sunny. There were many other families out today taking advantage of the good weather. And I noticed, several times, someone pushing an orange jogging stroller—the same type we had bought for Landon, which is now in a cardboard box in the basement.

Landon would be eight months today… Landon would be eight months today… Landon would be eight months today… That thought starts to play on a continuous loop through my mind.

So my happy times are always bittersweet now. There's always a missing piece, a hollow absence that can be felt no matter how much my heart is filled with love, no matter how brightly the sun shines. I'm not sure if that will ever change. I'm not sure if I want it to. That missing piece is Landon, and that absence I feel is my connection to him.

MARCH 18

> The worst part of holding the memories is not the pain. It's the loneliness. Memories need to be shared.
>
> —LOUIS LOWRY, *THE GIVER*

I remember thinking last fall that if I could just make it through until spring, I would be okay. Spring has always been my favourite season. The air is crisp and fresh and the warmth of the sun begins to thaw the frigid earth. Little bits of green start to push through the dirt, and everything becomes brighter and more alive.

This year the weather has warmed up earlier than usual. I tuned up my bike and have started to cycle commute everywhere again, which is one of my favourite things in the world. I forgot how much I love to feel the wind on my face.

But, of course, I find myself constantly reminded of last spring, my last trimester of pregnancy with Landon. This was the season when Landon was such a big baby already, kicking and squirming and rolling around inside my belly. There was new life and growth inside and out: everyday a new development, a new milestone, a new bud blossoming. All the mama birds were nesting too. Excitement and anticipation filled the air and every breath I took.

Spring was when I felt the most connected to my baby. Every morning as I walked Cody, Landon would be doing his own little exercise routine. His butt would poke out and make my belly look all weird and lopsided. He would stretch out and tickle me with his fingers while pushing his "giant" feet up into my ribs. I never felt alone. No matter what, he was always there with me.

Now that he's gone, these memories are all I have. And what's sadder is that nobody else got to know him as I did. Nobody else got to experience him when he was healthy and strong. All anyone else knows is brain-dead Landon, sick Landon, dying Landon.

MARCH 21

This has been an interesting week for me. "Intense" seems like a good way to describe it. And it's no wonder too, with yesterday being such a powerful, rare and auspicious day in astrological terms: the spring equinox, a total solar eclipse and a new moon (also a super moon) all coinciding. It's a major turning point, a start of a new cycle, a time to embrace new possibilities and let go of what is old and no longer working anymore.

Intuitively I feel as though something major is happening. I feel hopeful. Last night, I told Justin I had the feeling that if we were going to get pregnant, then it would be now, on the equinox. The start of a new moon cycle, the start of spring—

everything in me said that this might also mean the start of a new life. He thought this was pretty crazy but went along with it nevertheless.

This morning I went to a yoga class, and some interesting things happened there. First, an older woman I've never spoken to before approached me after class and told me I appeared to her in a vision during her practice. She saw me sitting across from her on my yoga mat surrounded by white light. Then the teacher, Amanda, whose classes I took all the way through my pregnancy with Landon, told me she had a gift for me. She had bought it a few months previous but was waiting for the right time to give it to me. I opened it up to find a children's book called *The Heart and the Bottle* by Oliver Jeffers. In the card she wrote that when she thinks of me and Landon, a strong image comes to her mind, one of me reading to two little children in a cozy room: one girl and one boy (Landon). The room is lit by what appears to be magical candlelight. When you look closely you see that the light is emanating from Landon.

Her words brought me to tears, as did the book. It is a touching story about a girl who loses someone she loves and decides to put her heart in a glass bottle to keep it safe. It seems to fix things, at first, but then she notices she is no longer filled with all the wonder and curiosity of the world. She tries to get her heart out of the bottle, but can't—she doesn't remember how. Until one day she meets a little girl, smaller and still curious about the world, who helps her put her heart back where it belongs. As I sat in my car after class reading the book, I was overwhelmed with emotion. I'm not sure why, but I have this strong sense that this book is a sign. Maybe a little girl is coming into my life? Maybe Landon will have a little sister one day?

MARCH 29

Are you holding your breath in? Taking tiny sips of air, just enough to get by? The way you breath is always a metaphor for how you are living your life. What are you attaching to, unable to let go of?

Exhale completely.
Let go of all your grasping.
Even if just for this one moment.
Pause in the emptiness.
Settle in to the calm.
Then, notice your inhale.
How much bigger and more expansive does it become?

The beauty of letting go is that you create empty space, ready and eager to be filled. Opportunities for new growth, healing—maybe new joy—rush in because they are all around you, waiting patiently to be let in.

APRIL 6

I used to love being with pregnant women. I was surrounded

by them during my teaching of prenatal yoga and during the time spent with pregnant friends and coworkers. I loved seeing their growing bellies, loved talking about names and due dates. To me there was nothing more beautiful and life-affirming than a radiant, expecting mom.

Now when I see a pregnant woman, I don't see a life-giving goddess, I see a ticking time bomb, and my heart starts to pound loudly and my throat tightens so much that I feel as though I'm suffocating. Panic, rage and deep sadness crash down on me like a giant wave. Having babies seems so easy and natural for them, and for me it feels like the hardest and scariest thing in the world. It takes all my effort to keep from breaking down.

What hurts the most is that these pregnant women are a constant reminder of everything I've lost, and also of all the fear I live with. Even when/if I get pregnant, I fear that I'll never get to feel again the pure joy of having a baby growing inside of me. I'll never be able to enjoy a baby shower or go to birth classes and chat excitedly with other moms. Others tell me that getting pregnant will make things better, but I'm not so sure. If it stresses me out so much to even be around pregnancy, how will I ever handle being pregnant again myself?

I'm not angry at other women for being pregnant. I can't expect the world to stop reproducing. But I do know they are a major trigger for my grief. It's even harder now because people assume by this time I would be getting better and moving on. Truth is, it gets harder every day that I'm further away from holding Landon and no closer to holding his sibling, all the while terrified and unsure if that's ever going to happen.

I'm going to have to find a way to cope, particularly since my sister-in-law is due with a baby boy close to Landon's birthday. But I'm torn. On one hand, I feel like I'll never be able to handle my anxiety around pregnant women (and new babies for that matter) so it's best if I avoid them. On the other hand, I realize this attitude is self-centred and would result in alienating the people I love. So do I protect myself but feel horribly selfish and even more isolated or do I stick it out in hopes things get better?

APRIL 7

I'm feeling immensely grateful for all the love and support that's been pouring in since my last post. Yesterday was a really hard day, but all the messages of empathy, compassion and hope from my online following lifted me up. My heart feels much lighter today knowing that so many care—and understand—what I'm going through. I've decided to speak my truth more openly and honour what I need, knowing that it might be a little different every day. I know others don't intend to hurt me, but they say or do hurtful things because they don't know how I'm truly feeling (and I really can't expect them to). So I've decided the best solution is to be really honest and clear to others about what I need and where I'm at in this crazy journey. If others can't understand or honour that, then that is okay too. Things fall together; things fall apart. The tides roll in and out. The water will always be calm after a storm.

APRIL 15

I often get emails from customers who love their PranaVidaStyle clothing, and this always brightens my day. One thing I never expected since re-launching in September is the way my clothing line has opened up conversations about baby loss. This is a story one of my customers, Wendy, sent to me yesterday:

> Amelia,
>
> Thank you.
> I received my order today (adult medium high waist leggings and child small leggings). They are beautiful. They fit superbly. They are awesome! More so, our little girl, Susanna, and I danced around in them pretending to be butterflies, because it made her happy. Every time we stopped, she begged for more, and so it went.
> Yet, we couldn't have had these moments of joy were it not for our postman, Rick, who delivered them. We happened to be outside when he came, and my husband told me the pants had arrived. We chatted a bit with Rick (he's a good man, the kind who you want in your life), and I shared with him

Landon's story.

Amelia, he paused. His face shifted to warm joy and gratitude. He shared that he had lost a son years ago to SIDS. He commended you on Landon's Legacy. Rick is the kind of man I want as a role model for our daughters. I had no idea of that part of his life until I shared your story. I believe his words were, "For anyone to take that and graciously make something positive of it is incredible."

I know your path isn't easy. I've seen my own family lose children at birth. I just want to thank you for what you are doing, even when it's not easy, fun, etc.

It warms my heart to hear about the ways Landon is still making a difference and is still remembered by many. In my darkest hours I try to remember this, and it always lifts me up. Thank you for listening, and thank you even more for sharing.

APRIL 28

Today I met a newborn baby. Not intentionally, but we crossed paths in the washroom at the doctor's office. I didn't notice she was there until I went to grab for a paper towel and almost ran into her carrier. She was wrapped in a pink blanket, half asleep, eyes partly open and looking rather goofy.

For the first time since Landon, I didn't look for a way to leave as quickly as possible upon seeing a healthy newborn.

I didn't feel an unbearable sadness or jealous rage boiling up inside. I actually talked to the mom briefly and admired the baby's cuteness. This was the first time I was able to say "congratulations!" and mean it.

I'm not sure why this baby wasn't the same emotional trigger as all the other babies I've seen since Landon died. I guess it's a good sign though, whatever the reason. And guess what? The baby's name was Lily.

APRIL 30

Last night it poured with rain: the first big rainfall of the spring. This morning I woke up earlier than usual, with a sense of energy and aliveness I haven't felt in a long time. Everything had turned green overnight, and I spotted the first blooms of the year—tulips and daffodils—sprouting from the earth. I feel this is a good sign.

MAY 2

Do you remember back in November when I wrote about a woman (an intuitive) who told me after taking my yoga class that she got the feeling that something big would happen in April? Ever since then I've been wondering, what did she mean? Will I find out I'm pregnant with Landon's brother or sister in April?

All this past month I've been eating so much and craving all the rich, high-calorie food I craved in my first trimester with Landon. I didn't want to get my hopes up, so I convinced myself this was because of stress. I also started to feel my belly getting bigger, but I told myself it was probably because of the overeating. Because I couldn't bear the thought of another negative pregnancy test, I decided not to take a test until I was almost certain, or until April 30th.

Finally April 30th rolled around and I decided to buy a test kit. I was still trying to convince myself I wasn't pregnant. After all, I still haven't had a period since Landon was born (we even have an appointment to see a fertility doctor next month). But my intuition told me I had to check, that maybe, just maybe, the woman was right and April would be the month.

So I peed on the stick. Right away one blue line appeared. Then a second line slowly started to appear. At this point I thought I was seeing things, until I looked again and realized the first bold, strong line was the one that meant I WAS PREGNANT!

I was in awe. I started to cry, with happiness. I never expected to feel that happy again. I thought I'd feel terrified, but no, this felt just right. Justin is over-the-moon excited and of course so are our family and friends.

I remember that with Landon I just wanted time to pass so I could feel him kick, get bigger, be born. Now I'm happy exactly where we are. I know any day things could change, so I'm determined to enjoy having our baby here with us, now. That's one of the many wonderful gifts Landon has given to us and his little brother or sister—the ability to slow down and enjoy what's happening in the here-and-now. And also courage—after surviving the loss of Landon I feel as though we are invincible. We have been through the worst possible thing, and we are still standing and smiling and learning to find joy in the middle of it all. I know that we would be absolutely devastated if we lost this baby too, but I know we would survive. And as with every life, however long or short, this life would have had a purpose. Some babies don't walk on the earth but they all leave their legacy in our hearts.

MAY 7

Dear Baby,

It's already been one whole week since we found out you are here with us. I hope you are enjoying yourself in there. It makes me happy knowing that you get to share the space your brother lived most of his life in.

Ever since your brother died, I've been wondering what it might be like to carry his little brother or sister. At first I felt that I could never love another baby the way I love your brother, and even the thought of having another baby to "heal" made me angry. I knew your brother could never be replaced that and there was nothing in the world that could mend together the million pieces my heart shattered into when I found out he wasn't going to come home with us.

All I wanted initially was to be Landon's mom. So I decided I would continue to mother Landon, just in different ways. I wouldn't be able to nurse him, but I could donate my milk. I wouldn't be able to do yoga with him, but I could host a yoga retreat for moms who lost babies. I wouldn't be able to watch him grow up, but I could tell his story and see him have a bigger impact than if he had lived one hundred years. And I will keep on being his mother for as long as I live.

But I also knew that once your brother got a bit "older," a bit more independent, I would be ready to give him a little sister or brother. This still scared me though—what if something went wrong? Could I survive losing another baby? Even though Daddy and I were trying to make you for a while, I intuitively knew that you wouldn't arrive until my heart was ready. I needed to get to a place in my healing where I felt that I was strong enough to handle anything and where I could love and trust myself again. And I think you knew that too.

I know I'll still have my bad days, but I am going to do everything I can to make sure Landon's legacy has only a positive impact in your life. I want you to be able to feel all my joy and excitement. I want you to come into this world surrounded by love, not fear. I know I thought I could never love another baby as much as I did Landon, but I was wrong, so wrong. I've just grown another heart so I can love you both equally.

Forever and Ever, Mom

MAY 8

Today would have been Landon's ten-month birthday. In the morning, I taught my yoga class as usual, and to my surprise the intuitive woman who had come to my class back in November, the one who predicted something big would happen in April, showed up. We started chatting and I asked her if she remembered what she'd told me. It took her a moment to recall, but she did remember and was delighted when I told her my news. She told me with certainty that everything was going to be okay. I could tell she wasn't just saying that to ease my nerves. She knew.

After the class, I was curious and wanted to know more. She reaffirmed again that this pregnancy and birth would go well. Then, after a moment of pause, she added that she was getting the sense that it will be very important that I *trust my intuition*. I'm not sure what she meant by this advice, but I hope it will make more sense in time.

Interestingly, just as she was leaving, she asked me, "Do you like to write?" Before I could answer, she said that she knew I was going to write two books—an autobiography or memoir, and another book. She told me that if I wasn't already, I should start writing a journal, and I should keep all of my writings in a safe place.

I'm not sure what to make of all this. I'm hesitant to write about this interaction because it all sounds so crazy, and I'm pretty skeptical about this kind of stuff. I've had the intention of writing a book ever since my talk with Trinette at the beach back in August. But since then I haven't really thought too much about it. Oddly enough, just last night I had a vivid dream that I was holding the finished book in my hands—I even remember what the cover image was. (It's a photo of me on a swing set at sunrise, which I took at Winnipeg Beach a few weeks after Landon died. I'd taken the photo using the self-timer on my iPhone while on an early morning walk with Cody. Only days later, when I was scrolling through my photos, did I notice the empty baby swing beside me. It gave me chills and I felt Landon's presence stronger than ever). I rarely remember my dreams, but this dream left a strong impression in my mind.

So maybe the universe is trying to tell me something? If there's one thing I've learned from Landon, it's that anything is possible. The worst of the worse, but also, maybe, the best of the best.

MAY 12

Dear Landon,

It's been ten months since we said goodbye. Soon it will be a whole year. And then I probably won't even count the months. It's so hard moving further and further away from our short time together, but I notice that, most days, that part of my life feels more "natural"; it has become part of who I am now, part of my story.

Daddy and I know you want us to be able to see your life, even though it was short, as one of the best things that ever happened to us. I know you want us to be happy that you lived, not sad that you died. I know you want us to delight in every moment we have with your siblings and to cherish them so much more now that we truly know nothing is for certain.

That doesn't change that we miss you more than anything, and it's hard as hell not to be able to parent you here on earth. We'll never stop wondering what you would look like or what you would be doing. We will always feel that we are missing one of us, no matter how much our little family grows.

But there's less sadness now when we talk about you. There is more joy and pride. You have done so much already, baby boy. We couldn't be more grateful you chose us to be your parents. We know that even though you couldn't stay, you are still teaching us and we are still growing. Oh, and the flowers on the apple tree we planted for you at your memorial have started to blossom! One day we'll gather apples with your siblings and tell them all about how special their big brother is. Our relationship will never end. So in that sense, you really are always with us.

Love always, Mom

MAY 15

This morning I had a dentist appointment, just a regular cleaning and checkup. The dental hygienist—a woman in her late forties, genuinely sweet and caring—was the same hygienist I'd had appointments with during and after my pregnancy with Landon. In fact, she was the same hygienist I had when I started going to the dentist as a little kid. My appointment back in October was definitely awkward, with her not knowing what she should say and with me, still so heavy with grief, fighting back tears behind those silly sunglasses. This time, it was nice to be able to tell her the good news of our new baby on the way. Her face just lit right up! She was genuinely excited and happy for us.

The mood quickly shifted though when just a few minutes into the appointment, she had to excuse herself to answer a phone call. I sensed that it was something urgent. When she returned, her eyes were full of tears and she looked terribly upset. She explained that she was finally getting the MRI results for her daughter, who had been suffering bad headaches and vision loss. I didn't want to ask questions or say much because I could tell how hard she was trying to keep it together and stay focused on her job. So I just said how sorry I was and told her she could take all the time she needed. I made my best effort to send all the love and good energy I could to her throughout the appointment. At one point she said, "Thank you, I know you understand." I wondered if it wasn't somehow meant to be, the way our paths connected again at this particular time.

Afterwards, I was at the front desk paying and the receptionist passed me a glass vase filled with a beautiful bouquet of flowers. Noticing the surprised look on my face, she explained, "Every Friday we give flowers to one of the patients. Your hygienist wanted you to have these today."

The flowers are mostly orange lilies—Landon's lilies. Coincidence? I don't know. What a crazy world—sometimes so terribly messed up and painful—but wonderfully beautiful all the same.

MAY 16

Today marks seven years since Justin and I became a couple.

When we met he was a skinny kid with a big heart and brilliant mind who could run like the wind. I was impressed that at the age of twenty he already knew exactly what he wanted and where he was headed. I was an intense runner too, but in the rest of my life I was insecure and unsure and had no idea what direction I wanted to go in. It was around the time we met that I started my yoga practice and slowly found—or fell onto—my path.

I remember thinking on our first date that he would be an amazing father. He has a natural enthusiasm for life and an imagination that rivals most three-year-olds. And having three younger siblings born when he was in his late teens, he's certainly no stranger to babies. I think he'll always be a child at heart—something that balances the aged soul in me. I've always felt far older than my years.

And he *is* an amazing father. I wish more than ever that we didn't have to become parents under the circumstances we did, but I do know that it has made us much stronger as a couple and as parents. There is nothing harder than being a parent to a child not on this earth and then opening your heart to love another child when you know there are no guarantees.

But when you do, you realize there is really nothing that can stand in your way. When you let go of fear and stop trying to shield yourself from pain, but rather let it move in and through you, it no longer has the power to shape and control your life. You stop wasting energy on protecting your sensitive spots and seeking ways to stop bad things from happening because you realize this is a far more painful burden than feeling the raw pain itself.

Rather than seeing a cruel world that is working against you, you open to a world that is actually working *for* you— conspiring to help you in your personal growth by shattering the walls you have worked hard to build and fortify. You begin to see a world that is not always easy but far more big and beautiful and generous than you could have imagined. In the words of Michael Singer, "Pain is the price you pay for freedom."

MAY 25

There are times I still feel unbelievably sad that Landon isn't alive; and there are times I feel unbelievably happy that he did live and is changing my life and so many others. Other times I'm just trying to wrap my head around the fact that there is another little human growing inside me, getting bigger every day. The moments it does sink in, I'm overwhelmingly grateful and in love with this little bean. But I'm still having a hard time thinking ahead to the future with any certainty. I'll say, "Next summer we'll have a six month old…" But in my mind I'm thinking *if we're lucky*.

Today I felt more hopeful though: I put away all the clothes I won't be able to wear again until after the baby comes. I took a prenatal yoga class. Baby steps.

MAY 31

Being pregnant with Landon seemed to go by so slowly, but this pregnancy seems to be flying by. Perhaps partly because I've done it all before, and partly because physically I feel so much better this time around. Baby's movements are getting more obvious now, and she/he seems to love raspberries and blueberries. Sometimes I'll eat a bowl full just so I can lie down and feel baby stretching and tickling me inside.

Landon didn't seem to like berries at all. I didn't get sick much, but I did once after eating a bowl of mixed berries and couldn't even look at them for the rest of my pregnancy. It's interesting how babies can be so different even at this size-of-a-lime stage, and noticing these differences does help—it reaffirms that this is a new pregnancy, with a new outcome. It gives me hope that this baby will get to come home with us.

JUNE 8

I'm feeling grateful to have Cody, especially on the hard days. Landon would have been eleven months today, and I bet he and Cody would have been best buds. Landon would probably be crawling (walking?) all over the place and Cody would have been such a gentle and protective "big brother." It breaks my heart knowing that they'll never get to explore this world together.

But I also know that Cody isn't wondering about the "what

ifs" and "should have beens." He isn't angry or jealous or sad. He's just enjoying every splendid moment he has, running at top speed through the fields and jumping into every body of water he can find, for no other reason than the pure joy of it. Sadness about the past or worries about the future don't cloud his mind or distract him from enjoying what's actually happening. He'll probably live a fuller life in his ten to fifteen years than most humans will in eighty. Cody reminds me what's really important: what we have right here, right now.

I know I'll never stop thinking about Landon, missing Landon and wondering who he would've been. But I also know that there is much I can accomplish, and many ways I can honour his memory, and one is by being really present with all of the wonderful things happening now. Because like it or not, my life as I know it now is because Landon is gone. To fully appreciate all the wisdom, connections and opportunities his life and death brought to this world, I need to fully appreciate all of life as it is—not what I hoped it would be, not what I thought it would be or what I was told it would be—all of it, just as it is.

JUNE 13

It's here at last! The first Landon's Legacy Healing Retreat begins tomorrow. It was just nine months ago that the idea was first conceived, and now, after many months of planning and connecting with other bereaved moms, it has finally arrived! Organizing and preparing for this retreat have already been healing for me. It has given me something to look forward to and focus my energy on.

I've definitely gone through many periods of self-doubt too, wondering what the heck I'm getting myself into. How am I going to support other women going through this when I'm still trying to figure things out for myself?

But still I'm feeling much stronger and more confident these days. I feel that this week is going to be such an incredibly transformative one, for me and for the twenty-four moms coming from all over the United States and Canada, as well as from Mexico, Germany and Sweden. I'm excited to meet everyone. The moms have already been connecting on Facebook for the past few months, so by the time we meet it'll feel like a big reunion. Yesterday was a busy day making all the final preparations, tonight there will be a dinner with the early arrivals and tomorrow we make our way to the Whiteshell for a healing week of yoga, counselling, meditation, hiking, walking the beach and just being with each other.

I'm truly feeling blessed by all the support we've received since the beginning. With fundraising yoga classes and the GoFundMe.com campaign, we raised enough to help finance almost half of the participants' costs through the Landon's Legacy scholarship fund. This wouldn't have happened without all of the support and connections I've made through this wonderful online community, and I couldn't be more grateful.

JUNE 15

Everything has come together perfectly. All twenty-four moms made it here without any travel delays at all, and it's been incredibly wonderful to finally meet them in person. It's great, for once, not to feel like an outsider—to feel, instead, completely understood.

Another amazing aspect of this retreat is how nature seems to be supporting us in a huge way. It leaves me with no doubt that our babies are present here with us. All of Sunday was gorgeous, warm and sunny, perfect for our lunch in Assiniboine Park and the drive out to the resort. In the evening we had our opening circle, and just as we were introducing our babies and sharing their photos and memorabilia, the sky opened up with a massive thunderstorm—the first of the year. As our hearts opened and emotion and tears poured out, Mother Nature released her pent up energy along with us. Then, as we arranged the pictures and memorabilia of our babies on the altar in front of the windows overlooking the lake, the sun emerged and offered us a beautiful vibrant orange and pink sunset. It was as if our children were smiling down on us.

This morning was cloudy and cool, the perfect kind of weather for getting cozy and slowing right down, which was perfect for today's theme of "grounding." All of our *asanas*, *pranayama* and meditations centred around relieving issues relating to imbalances of the root or *manipura chakra*, one of the seven main *chakras* or "energy centres" in the human body according to yogic philosophy. Imbalance in this area can be caused by the fear, anxiety and sense of disconnectedness that come with grief and can also be especially intense when travelling to a new place and embarking on a new adventure. In the afternoon, Dawn, Ariana's mom, whom I met back in December, guided us through a wonderful mindful self-compassion workshop.

I can't help but feel our children are orchestrating things to line up just perfectly for us so that we know that they are *here* with us and that we are, without question, completely loved, completely protected, and completely supported.

JUNE 16

Today's intention or theme was "Open." We explored imbalances of the sacral or *svadhishthana chakra*, such as the loss of creativity, intimacy, passion and zest for life, or the inability to release inhibitions and "go with the flow" that often accompanies grief. Seeking pleasure or feeling pleasure often brings on a sense of guilt when we are grieving. This morning we enjoyed a fluid dance-inspired vinyasa class, working on specifically opening up the hips and lower back. Then we journaled or painted and did our compassionate sharing and listening. At the very end of the morning session, a butterfly flew up to the window, fluttered around a little as if trying to peek in, and then flew away. We were all in awe; that was the first butterfly anyone had seen during the retreat.

Fittingly, the butterfly is one of the most enduring symbols of human transformation. The caterpillar goes through a massive amount of transition during a short time in its cocoon to emerge anew as a beautiful butterfly. Before transformation, the caterpillar lives in a completely different world than it will as a butterfly and is unaware of the miraculous transformation it's about to undergo. Yet it seems to embrace the changes of its environment and body with unwavering acceptance; therefore, the butterfly is also symbolic of enduring faith, and it inspires us to surrender to the natural flow of life and turning tides of nature. It was as if the butterfly that came to the window just knew that we were moving, dancing, creating, flowing and opening and that, one breath at a time, we will also emerge transformed.

In the afternoon, we visited the Bannock Point petroforms, a sacred site nearby that I'd heard about but had never been to myself. My friend and fellow yoga teacher, Niki, who is very passionate about the site and visits often to make offerings, took us there. The petroforms are rocks that have been gathered and then arranged in various shapes, such as turtles, snakes and humans, and are found at several sites throughout the Whiteshell. Archaeologists have difficulty dating and interpreting petroforms because they consists of stones placed on a bare rock surface and have not been covered with soil over time like most archaeological sites. However, it is thought that the builders were pre-tribal aboriginal peoples (a generic people before they divided into distinct tribes) and that they were built for spiritual, healing, astronomical and teaching purposes. Today, the sites are sacred spaces primarily used by the Anishinabe (also known as Ojibway) people of the area, but groups have arrived from as far away as Minnesota, Wisconsin and Colorado to conduct traditional ceremonies. The Bannock Point petroform site is one of the only ones that is open to the public and happens to be located just a few miles from the retreat centre.

Quite serendipitously, as we entered the petroform site, a man named Ron appeared. He has been involved in protecting the area and teaching others about it for about thirty years. I'd heard about him but we'd never met before, so it was purely luck that we ran into him. He offered to give us a guided tour of the petroforms. Before actually visiting the rock formations, we all made medicine bundles and left tobacco offerings, then did walking meditation barefoot around the perimeter of the temple of trees that lies at the centre of the grounds. I'd never before felt Landon's presence so strongly. As I was walking, I had the tiniest baby chipmunk scurry right up to me. It kept playing around the rocks that circle the temple as I walked.

We then built a campfire and did a smudge with sage grass to cleanse ourselves of any negative energy. Ron told us many amazing things about the area and the many medicinal plants that grow there, as well as some of the magical things that have happened over the decades. One was that just today, butterflies started to appear. These are the keepers of the spirits of children who have passed, he said. Just then, we noticed a beautiful little butterfly on the ground. Surprisingly, it didn't fly away when we moved closer. It actually rested there for at least fifteen minutes, so everyone could get a look. Eventually I knelt down and got up close to it, and it fluttered right onto my arm. It stayed there for a bit, did a little dance around, and then left. How amazing is that?

One of the petroforms we visited was of a pregnant woman. There is a fascinating story about how this stone formation came to be. At one time it was a turtle, and had been for many, many years. Then one day Ron noticed the stones had changed to an outline of a body of a pregnant woman. He changed the stones back to form a turtle, but the next day they had changed back to represent a pregnant woman. This happened again a third time, and so he decided to camp out overnight beside the rocks he had arranged again in the shape of a turtle to see if he could see what was going on. During the night he woke up, startled by a noisy rattling and shaking sound. He lit up his flashlight to illuminate the petroform and saw that it had again changed back to the shape of a pregnant woman. He fell back asleep, and in his dream a woman appeared to him. She told him he should leave the rocks in the shape of a pregnant woman. They had changed that way to honour a woman who spent a lot of time there, a woman who had lost a baby during childbirth.

After telling this story, Ron said that on many occaisons he has guided a group into this space, someone starts crying—often that's a mother who has lost a child.

It was a powerful experience for all of the moms to hear that story and be in that space. It was a reminder that we do not and never will suffer alone. Millions of mothers for millions of years have been in our shoes.

JUNE 17

Today, our intention is to "empower." We are exploring issues related to the solar plexus or *manipura chakra* that so often accompany grief: a sense of weakness or powerlessness; a lack of self-confidence; a tendency to be overly self-critical, reactive and stressed out; and a tendency to either over-eat or under-eat.

This chakra is where I have had my greatest imbalance, but it is also where I've had the most growth and breakthroughs along my healing journey. I remember thinking of the idea of the retreat back in September but then thinking, *No way! I can't do that. Who would want to come? What if I don't match up to their expectations?* Throughout the next nine months, especially when regaining my strength and re-igniting my handstand practice in Thailand, I slowly gained more confidence that I *could* do hard things. I still had many moments of self-doubt, but more and more I started to believe—I *can* do things that scare me, I can do things that take me way out of my comfort zone.

Today we did a group activity with Niki where we had to write down one thing we were struggling with, then put the opposite of that in an "I am" statement. I wrote "self-consciousness," and my opposite statement was "I AM CONFIDENT." Then, we all lifted each mom up by the legs and she had to shout as loud as possible "I AM…" and fill in whatever was the opposite to her negative view. I felt so nervous and silly I didn't want to do it, so I was the last one to go. My first attempt was so weak they made me try again, and this time I said it loudly: "I AM CONFIDENT!" It wasn't easy, but maybe, just maybe, I'm starting to believe it.

This afternoon, we went for a hike to Pine Point Rapids, which is near the petroforms we visited yesterday. This place holds many memories for me. The first time Justin and I did this hike was actually the week Landon was conceived, and we went many times throughout my pregnancy. Since Landon was born, I'd only been back once.

Along the way I chatted with Tiffany, one of the first moms I connected with after Landon died. Her baby girl, Emma Grace, was stillborn at thirty-nine weeks, just ten days after Landon, and she is also now pregnant with her rainbow baby. While we were walking, she told me about how an orange butterfly had come to her when she came home from the hospital after delivering her baby. She wasn't able to go into the house at first, but this butterfly hung out with her in the yard until she felt strong enough to go in. I told her about the orange butterfly that had visited us at the petroforms the day before when she had stayed back because of feeling ill. We were both disappointed that she hadn't been there to witness that magical moment.

Just then we noticed that the same type of orange butterfly seemed to be following us. Once we got to the falls, the butterfly flew up to us and landed on my pink "Queen B Project" bracelet that Tiffany makes to raise funds for the non-profit she started in honour of Emma. The butterfly stayed with us for about thirty minutes, just flitting around, landing on our hands and feet. It seemed as if the butterfly was posing for us, almost as though it knew we wanted to have a photo with it.

JUNE 18

The theme for the final day of the retreat was "feel." This was the most intensely emotional day, where we focused on issues related to the heart or *anahata chakra*, which is the chakra most deeply affected by grief. This is why when we grieve, we literally feel like our hearts are broken, crushed or ripped right out. In the morning, we moved through a heart-opening yoga class accompanied by songs from our retreat playlist (a selection of songs, suggested by the moms, that they felt had connected them to their children or had been a significant part of their grieving and healing journeys). There were many tears, but the good kind—tears of release, tears of gratitude and tears of love for the children we lost.

In the evening, we gathered together on the beach for a closing ceremony that my friend and Ayurvedic counsellor, Kalee, guided us through. We arranged all of our children's photos and memorabilia on an altar we made on the beach, then we created a mandala with ten different kinds of seeds and grains, taking turns adding to it as we all chanted this mantra we'd learned:

Om poornam-adah poornam-idam poorna-aat
poornam-udachyate
Poorna-asya poornam-aadaaya poornam-evaa vashishyate
Om shaantih shaantih shaantih

(Om. This is whole and complete, That is whole and complete. This and That are whole and complete.
From wholeness comes wholeness.
When a portion of wholeness is removed, that which remains continued to be whole and complete.
Om, peace peace peace)

The words and meaning of this chant resonate strongly with me. It reminds me that even though Landon is not living, he is not gone. His life was whole and complete. Even though sometimes I feel broken, empty or as though a piece of me is missing, I am still whole. I am complete.

The mandala making and chanting lasted for at least

forty-five minutes. It was meditative and soothing, and the energy we created in that circle was incredibly powerful. We were all focused on the chant and mandala; we completely disconnected from what was going on in our surroundings. When the mandala was finished and we emerged from this almost trance-like state, we were in for a little surprise…

We had a visit from a fox! I've never in my life seen a fox so close. Some of the moms had sightings of a fox throughout the week, but just briefly and then it would run into the woods. This fox stayed around for at least thirty minutes. It was almost as if it wanted to see what we were up to.

One of the moms looked up fox symbolism and turns out that in China, a fox sighting is thought to be a signal from the spirits of the deceased. It is also thought that when a fox crosses your path, it can be a signal to open your eyes, so that you can see the situation for what it is—not as you wish it to be. This animal's agile movements remind us to be fluid and adaptable when a situation or an environment is difficult.

I like to think that our babies have been trying to send us all these signs to let us know they are really with us. Of course, they also sent us a beautiful sunset for our final night—complete with two tiny rainbows (or sun-dogs) reflecting on either side of the sun. We made an offering of flower petals to the lake and wrote our children's names in the sand. Afterwards we had a bonfire, roasted marshmallows for s'mores and talked late into the night. It was the *perfect* closing night.

JUNE 19

During the hike we went on to Pine Point Rapids earlier in the week, the group I was with had gotten separated from the rest for a portion of the walk. Afterwards, the other moms told me about an orange lily they had seen growing along the path, and I felt I couldn't leave the retreat without seeing it for myself. So early this morning, before heading back to Winnipeg, Tiffany and I returned to that hiking path to look for it. I was doubtful it would still be there, but I felt intuitively that I needed to go anyway.

About one kilometre into the hike we crossed a footbridge and came to a hilly area of solid rock. We were just about to turn back, thinking that the blooms had probably fallen off since the others saw them, when I spotted it. The lily was a single narrow stem growing right out of the rock. It had two blooms, still perfect and un-wilted. I've never seen a lily growing in the wild like this, especially not in a rock. The only other plants growing around it were moss and lichen and a bit of grass.

I don't know why I hadn't seen it when we hiked by the first time—it was so bright and close to the path. It was orange too, as all "Landon's lilies" that have shown up have been (interestingly, this is also the colour associated with the sacral chakra, which relates to fertility and pregnancy). But I think perhaps I was meant to see it on the last day. Maybe this was Landon's way of saying, *Good job Mama!*

On our walk back, our orange butterfly visited us again

one last time. We also saw a fox dart across the path. All of this made up a wonderful goodbye.

JUNE 27

With Landon's birthday just around the corner, my mind keeps travelling back to my final days of pregnancy with him. I was excited—and so blissfully naïve. No one had ever told me that babies can die for no reason and with no warning. But then, if someone had, I wouldn't have believed them. Or at least I wouldn't have believed it could happen to me.

I remember people asking me if I was nervous or scared at all for his birth, and quite honestly I never was. My body was designed to create, nurture and give birth to new life, and it had never failed me before. At twenty-five years of age and healthier in mind and body than I'd ever been, I never thought for a moment that it would fail me during pregnancy.

Now people ask if I'm anxious at all about this pregnancy and birth. And while I thought I would be a wreck, the truth is that so far I'm feeling pretty good. I've been trying to understand for a while why this is so. How can I be so calm knowing that any moment the worst thing imaginable could indeed happen, all over again? It occurred to me that maybe that's because I realize now that my body never did "fail." It still did everything it needed to do—everything it was designed to do. I still gave birth to a beautiful baby boy who is perfect in every way. *I don't think Landon's life was meant to be long, but I do think it was meant to be big.*

JUNE 30

Dear Baby,

Wow! it's been two whole months since the day we found out you are with us. But to be honest, I sensed you from the day you were conceived. It was the spring equinox, the new moon, and the eclipse that night. I could feel it deep in my heart that you and Landon would be choosing a really special time for you to come earth-side. And it couldn't have been any more perfect because, guess what? Your due date is December 11, my birthday!

I'm sorry I haven't given you as much attention as I'd like to lately. I've been busy focusing on your big brother and planning a retreat with his friends' moms. But now that you are getting a bit bigger, I'm noticing your tiny tickles more and more. Today I started to feel you are getting stronger—I can even feel your little kicks! Your dad and I love seeing your adorable little hands and feet, and your precious face (so cute already!) whenever we get to peek into your world through the ultra sound at the doctor's office.

Last appointment, our doctor found out if you are a boy or a girl! But we got him to seal that news in an envelope, and we vowed no peeking allowed (except for Auntie Alissa, who is planning the reveal). Your dad had the idea to save the surprise for Landon's birthday party. I like that idea. It will help us look forward to this day more and not be so sad because of not having Landon with us. So, as hard as it is not to know, we are going to wait. We are thinking of a piñata for the reveal, or maybe balloons or cupcakes? What do you think Landon will like more?

I hope you are growing healthy and strong and loving every minute of your time in my belly. What does it feel like to hear my heart beating from the inside? Can you hear us talking? Can you feel what I'm feeling? Are you just as excited to meet us as we are to meet you? Or do you already know us, and your birth will be just like coming home? I can't wait to actually hold you in my arms, hear you cry and look into your beautiful eyes.

I love you, Mom

JULY 6

I was in a crafty mood tonight. I decided to make a surprise lantern for baby's gender reveal on the 8th. I needed some beads and remembered a little pouch of them one of my students gave me not long after Landon died. It was filled with different kinds of beads and pendants, some with letters and symbols. She told me they spelled something, but I would have to put it together—like a puzzle. I had intended to, but, like many things at that time, it got put to the side and ended up at the bottom of Landon's memory box.

So today I finally dug it out of the box and pieced together the words. "Landon" and "July" were easy. The third word, "December," caught me off guard. Why December? She couldn't have known back then that Landon's sibling would be due in December. And what are the chances that I would only put the beads together now, right after finding out our baby's due date?

Maybe it's just some weird coincidence. But maybe it's

exactly how everything is meant to be. I love getting all these little signs, always when I need them the most. It's hard to be hopeful some days, especially with so many unknowns and "what ifs," but I can't help but feel like my little boy is watching over and making sure I know things are going to be okay.

JULY 7

Landon's lilies are in full bloom! It used to sadden me that I'd only get to enjoy their vibrant colour for such a short time, that only days after reaching their fullest bloom they would begin to wither and fall to the ground. Now, I don't mind. I think their short blooming lives make me appreciate them that much more. I don't pay a lot of attention to any of my other flowers. They are around most of the summer and are pretty enough, but they don't stand out in the same way.

I think of Landon as my little lily flower sometimes. He came and left so quickly, but in the time he was here he definitely made a powerful impression—one that will forever be etched in my memory and deep in my heart (and the hearts of so many others).

JULY 8

One year...

A year ago, I was certain I would always be broken. My heart felt as though it had shattered into a million pieces. My body felt as though it had been ripped in half then crudely stitched back together again. There was no way I could heal from that, I was certain. There was no way I could be happy again and no way I could smile or laugh again—no way I could live the rest of my life without my son. There was no way my body would ever move or feel the same way it did before the C-section. There was no way I would learn to trust my body again, and no way I could ever trust this world again—no way I could risk getting pregnant again, because that would mean risking losing another child. Of these things I was sure.

And yet here I am, one year later. Landon's little sister or brother is happily wriggling around in my belly, and I'm stronger than I ever thought possible. Turns out the broken pieces do start to mend together, with time and patience. The empty spaces do start to fill up again. Life isn't the way I thought it would be, and it's not the way I wanted it to be, but it's the life that chose me. Landon chose me. And I wouldn't have it any other way.

We decided to have Landon's birthday and the baby's gender reveal at my parents' house, the place where Justin and I were married. For the reveal, we even tied the surprise lantern from the very same tree that we stood under to exchange our vows on that sunny late summer evening almost four years ago. It was special to share these big moments with all of our family and friends in a place that is very dear to me, along the river where I spent much of my time while growing up and where I always felt the most connected to nature.

During the afternoon, just before heading over, I went out into my garden to pick a flower to pin in my hair. I wanted one of Landon's lilies but was disappointed to find that all of the orange blossoms had already withered or fallen to the ground. My yellow lilies had just started to bloom though, so I chose one of those instead. I didn't think much about it at the time, but it occurred to me later how perfect this all was. Yellow is joyful and bright, like the rising sun. It felt as though it was Landon's way of saying, *It's okay Mama, this day doesn't have to be all about me. You don't have to be so sad that I'm gone. You can be happy for this new baby!* And interestingly, yellow is associated with the solar plexus chakra, linked to strength, fearlessness and personal growth. Maybe Landon's sibling's lilies will be yellow.

When we arrived at my parents' house, the first things that caught my eye (after the lovely balloons and decoration!) were orange lilies in my parent's garden. I didn't remember there ever being orange lilies there before, so my first thought was that my mom planted them for Landon. I asked her about that, and she said no, these lilies she planted back in 1997 (the year of the flood of the century) after the garden was rebuilt. But for nearly twenty years they had been an off-white/cream colour.

"You won't believe what happened!" she said excitedly. Upon returning from a camping trip a few days ago, she was surprised to see that the lilies had come into full bloom—but this year, they were bright orange!

I just love the ways things keep showing up that remind us of Landon. It's as though he really wants to assure us that he's a part of all these special moments.

Well—it's a GIRL!!! My sister did a great job keeping the big secret until the reveal, but somehow deep down inside I just *knew*. Whenever I thought about, dreamed about or talked about this baby, I envisioned my little girl. Even Justin had a strong feeling we would have a girl. So our little Lily she was, from the very start. But nevertheless, it was the most exciting and incredible moment of pure joy as we watched the pink confetti and chocolates tumble from the surprise lantern to the ground.

Just then, I glanced down and noticed a few smooth, translucent blue and purple glass stones slightly buried in the earth. I recognized them immediately: they were the exact stones we used as paperweights to keep the marriage documents from blowing away in the breeze. They were still there after four years! They hadn't moved, not even a few feet, despite the yearly spring flood water rising far above this point and normally sweeping away any debris lying in its path.

So much has changed for Justin and me since that wonderful day four years ago, when we were happy, carefree and innocent—completely unaware of the loss and pain we would endure. To me the stones were a reminder that some things never change—like our love for each other, which despite the highs and lows, storms and swift currents, remains steadfast, solid and strong.

JULY 12

I give you this one thought to keep -
I am with you still - I do not sleep.
I am a thousand winds that blow,
I am the diamond glints on snow,
I am the sunlight on ripened grain,
I am the gentle autumn rain.
When you awaken in the morning's hush,
I am the sweet uplifting rush,
of quiet birds in circled flight.
I am the soft stars that shine at night.
Do not think of me as gone -
I am with you still in each new dawn.

—NATIVE AMERICAN PRAYER

Dear Landon,

It's hard to believe that it's been one whole year since we last held you in our arms. A year since that moment when your whole squishy body pressed up against my chest and you finally decided to let go. A year since you took your last sweet breath. A whole year since that agonizing day when we had to leave you there at the hospital, cold and lifeless.

I remember that awful car ride home all too clearly. I screamed every time we went over a bump or pothole because of the pain from the

C-section. But that was nothing compared to pain of the emptiness I felt inside of me. You were as much a part of me as my heart, my lungs, my stomach. How could I live without you? It just didn't seem possible.

But, somehow, we've managed to live on, and now we're finding comfort in celebrating your birthday. That was the day we got to see your precious face for the first time. We got to count your fingers and toes and marvel over what a good-lookin' newborn you were. Even though I knew there was no hope you would survive, getting to meet you after those long nine months of anticipation trumped the agony of knowing that hello was also goodbye.

But how do we get through the anniversary of the day you died? One of your angel friends, Paisley, has a very strong mom who helped by reminding me that the definition of "dead" is "spiritless." Your body is lifeless, yes, but you, Landon, were and never will be "spiritless." You are everywhere. You are everything. You live in our thoughts and hearts. And you are letting us know how close you really are. So maybe this isn't so much an anniversary of your death as an anniversary of your departure. You are gone from our arms, but never gone very far.

Love you always, Mom

JULY 15

Lately, despite my initial lack of anxiety, I've been feeling more and more anxious about this pregnancy. I think it has to do with approaching the halfway point. Although she was our precious Lily from the time we found out she was with us, I find now that I love her more and more every day. Lily isn't just in my imagination anymore—she is a real, wriggling and kicking baby. This whole thing is slowly becoming more and more real—and more and more scary.

My rational mind knows that complications during birth that lead to the baby dying are very, very rare (about one in every 1,000 in North America). So there is next to no chance of that happening again for us, especially with all the extra care and attention we'll be getting. But at the same time, there's that part of me that just is not totally convinced. What if there is something wrong with me? How does anyone know for sure? And not only that worry, but what about the things that Lily could die from that are more common than what happened to Landon: stillbirth, SIDS? I know people say lightning doesn't strike twice… but it does. I've met moms who have lost more than one baby or child. It really doesn't seem humanly possible to go through that much suffering more than once, but they do.

So yes, sometimes I feel hopeful, sometimes I feel strong. Then sometimes, usually halfway between sleep and waking, when my brain lets its guard down and I can't talk myself out of feeling fears, I just start crying. But I tell myself that's okay. I'd much rather have someone to cry over (the possibility of) losing, than no one at all.

It's tempting to want to just push those negative thoughts or worries away. Especially in the yoga community, it's common to hear teachers say things like, "Let go of any negative thoughts" or "think positive—your thoughts and emotions have a direct effect on your health/physical body." While this is great advice to a certain degree, it can also be very troubling and confusing. How does someone suffering from depression just "let go" of all negative thoughts? How can people with cancer accept that maybe their disease occurred because they weren't thinking positively enough? Does this mean that those of us who are pregnant should try to *never* have fears and "what ifs" because we might affect our unborn children in a bad way by being too negative or anxious?

I think it's important to remember that sometimes bad shit *just happens*. After all, I thought nothing *but* positive thoughts with Landon. It hadn't occurred to me that something might go wrong until I woke up from the surgery and he wasn't there. Also, there is an important distinction between attaching to negative emotions and expressing them. Expressing emotion intentionally in words, written or spoken, is one of the most effective ways of actually releasing some of the negative stuff that can weigh us down, creating a heavy burden to bear over time. Sometimes we can get so concerned about projecting a certain "Zen" image of ourselves that we don't allow ourselves to express the real anger, confusion or anxiety we feel. It bottles up inside and eventually starts to spill out in all sorts of messy and unwelcome ways.

So rather than trying to feel a certain way, I think it's important to be completely honest with yourself: How do you *really* feel? Say it, write it, yell it. Better out than in. And know that it is perfectly okay—no, it's *more* than okay—to *not always* be up and positive.

JULY 23

Lately I've noticed that I can "naturally" feel much more positive and hopeful. There are so many things that convince me Landon must be watching out for us. Lily was conceived on the spring equinox, is due on my birthday, and—get this—her due date is only two days apart from that of Trinette's baby!

Trinette and I had always hoped to have babies around the same time. Back in early April, on Landon's nine-month birthday actually, we went for a walk in Bird's Hill Park (where Landon's chickadees hang out). Near the end of the walk, she started telling a long story about a dream she had, about three babies and them talking to each other. I knew right away what she was trying to say, but I could tell she didn't know how to bring it up. Eventually I couldn't contain my excitement anymore. "YOU'RE PREGNANT!!" I blurted out.

I was surprised by how happy this made me. In some ways it felt as though Trinette was getting her rainbow baby. Even though she's never lost a baby, she went through so much of what I went through alongside me, on top of losing her dad to cancer over the winter. She also has a unique perspective as a rainbow baby herself. Her oldest brother, Anders, died over thirty years ago in a tragic accident at five months old. Even though she never met him, she grew up thinking about him and wondering what life would be like had he lived.

Today, we spent the afternoon at the beach. It occurred to me that last summer we had done the same thing—walking on the beach and talking; that's when we started discussing the idea of my writing Landon's story. This time it was cloudy and drizzled with rain occasionally, but we didn't care. We wrapped ourselves in blankets and I read out loud what I have written of my book so far. It was therapeutic to relive the past year in words and to see just how far I've come.

When I lost Landon, I lost a part of myself. But that hole, the empty void his loss carved out, also made space for me to be filled with other things. He taught me lessons that otherwise might have taken me a lifetime to learn. He taught me to cherish each moment, each breath, each relationship. He taught me to honour my body and appreciate all that it can do, not dwell on the things it can't do. He taught me to appreciate the little things in life and to find joy and beauty everywhere. He taught me that there are no mistakes, no coincidences. Everything is a miracle, and everything has its purpose. We just have to open our hearts and trust that we can one day understand what that purpose is. As much as losing Landon filled me with a sorrow greater than I had ever experienced, it also gave me strength I never thought existed and opened me to the possibility of creating a richer, more beautiful life in his honour. For this I am very, very grateful.

One year ago I could never have imagined I'd be where

I am today. But here I am. I survived. But more than that, Landon's story has created a ripple of hope and healing in the world, a legacy that wouldn't have existed had he not lived and died. *Landon's Legacy*. I sure am proud I get to be his mom.

LILY'S BIRTH

It is understood that the beauty of a rainbow does not negate the ravages of any storm. When a rainbow appears, it does not mean that the storm never happened or that we are not still dealing with its aftermath. It means that something beautiful and full of light has appeared in the midst of the darkness and clouds. Storm clouds may still hover, but the rainbow provides a counterbalance of colour, energy and hope.

—UNKNOWN

Lily's birth story is a beautiful one with a happy ending, but there are parts that were incredibly difficult. The two days leading up to Lily's birth brought to light the probable cause of Landon's death and were some of the scariest days of my entire life. I was hesitant at first to share my experience online, as I was worried people might blame me or my doctors for not preventing what happened to Landon. But I decided to share my experience in hopes that it empowers other women to listen to their bodies and intuition and advocate for themselves and their babies in whatever ways feel right. The response I received was overwhelmingly positive, and Landon's story has ended up having an even bigger impact that I ever imagined possible.

NOVEMBER 20

It's 11 p.m. Tonight is the last night I'll have Lily inside me. Thank goodness she is just as lively as ever, kicking and stretching like crazy. I know I should sleep, but I can't. Her moving isn't keeping me up—*I'm just so scared it will stop.*

Two nights ago I awoke just after midnight. I had a prickly, itchy feeling all over my body but mainly on my legs and feet. The itch was mild but very familiar. In an instant I knew something was wrong. I remembered the same kind of itch started at this stage of my pregnancy—thirty-seven weeks—with Landon, and got more severe in the weeks following. (Back then, I didn't at first think too much of it, since itchiness is a common symptom in the third trimester, usually attributed to stretching skin and increased estrogen levels. And after all, I was healthy and young and was told I had a textbook-perfect pregnancy. I have no family history of pregnancy-related health issues. I'd never even had so much as a cold or headache in over eight years! I mentioned my itching at my weekly doctor appointments a couple times but was told again this was normal. I remember a fleeting feeling that something was not right, but then I convinced myself that this must be just what many women experience in the third trimester.) In my still half-sleeping state, the intuitive woman (who predicted my pregnancy with Lily) came to mind. I recalled the conversation we had the second time we met, in early May, shortly after I found out I was pregnant. "Just make sure to trust your intuition," she had said.

Those words kept running through my head over and over until I got out of bed, sat down at my computer, and read through every single medical journal article and website I could find on pregnancy itchiness. I learnt that not only do I have the main symptom—itching without a rash—of a liver disease know as intrahepatic cholestasis of pregnancy (ICP), but also I have other symptoms, which I also had when pregnant with Landon: pain just below the right side of my rib cage (I thought that was just pressure from baby's feet; dark urine (I thought baby was just taking my fluids and I needed to drink more water); and lack of appetite (I figured my stomach was shrinking as baby took up more space). I read case study after case study of babies who had died suddenly and unexpectedly, either shortly before or during birth, because of this disease. While it is more common that the baby dies before birth (stillbirth), some stories were remarkably similar to what happened to Landon—acute fetal asphyxia during labour not due to an obvious reason like a cord accident.

It's not known exactly what causes ICP, but current research suggests genetic and hormonal factors. It affects about 1 percent of pregnant women in North America. There is no risk to mom, but if undiagnosed there is about a 15 percent chance of stillbirth or perinatal death and more than 30 percent chance of serious complications for baby. Almost all deaths occur after thirty-six weeks gestation. There is also a 70 to 90 percent likelihood the disease will recur in subsequent pregnancies. There is no way to detect it with fetal monitoring and ultrasounds, only by liver-function and bile-acid-level blood tests that aren't normally done. The good news—if diagnosed, medicated with Ursodiol and if baby is delivered early (by thirty-six to thirty-seven weeks), the risk of the baby dying or having complications drops to that of average healthy pregnancies.

By the time the next morning arrived I knew we needed to go to the hospital. I woke up Justin and we drove for two hours (usually a twenty minute drive) through a snowstorm and grid-lock traffic to the hospital (Winnipeggers tend to forget how to drive at the start of every winter). My doctor wasn't there that morning but referred us to an excellent high-risk obstetrician. We discussed my concerns and decided to start medication, get blood tests, and meet the next day to make a plan.

After another sleepless night, we went back to the hospital this afternoon and found out that, as I expected, my liver function test levels are elevated—suggesting that, along with my symptoms, I likely did/do have ICP. The total serum, bile acid-level test that will confirm this diagnosis will take at least a week or two to get back, since there are only a few labs in North America that run this test. Although there is no way of proving this is what caused Landon's death, and the doctors are only able to say at this point that it is "probable" I have/ had ICP, I'm not about to wait around to find out for sure. I know something is wrong, and I feel very strongly that Lily needs to be born as soon as possible. *I've never been so sure about anything in my life.*

We were given two options: having a C-section tomorrow morning, or waiting a few days to get induced. Although earlier in my pregnancy I was feeling more positive and fearless about giving birth, now I was feeling overwhelmed. I'm still haunted by memories of the operating room from when we lost Landon, and the excruciating pain of my infection and recovery afterwards. I'm afraid that going through the physical pain of a C-section again will bring me back to the intensity of the emotional pain. But I also know induction isn't a good option, as that will be even more stressful. Physically, I have a slightly increased risk of uterine rupture because of my prior C-section, and this risk is increased if labour is induced. Emotionally, I can't wait a few days—and I don't trust that Lily will be safe inside me for a few more days. I haven't slept in over forty-eight hours and know I won't be able to sleep until she is born.

With all the risks and unknowns already stacked against us, plus the fact that most of the doctors and labour and delivery nurses at the hospital still remember Landon, it quickly became clear to me that my hopes of a natural vaginal birth were out the window. I decided that to get Lily out as fast and safely as possible and to eliminate the possibility of having to endure another crash C-section, the best option would be to have an elective C-section. We were told to come back at eight the next morning and they would get us in to the operating room as soon as possible. I still feel a bit scared, but more so very relieved. At this point, my fear of losing Lily has become much more intense than my fear of surgery. I would do anything to make sure she is born safe.

Lily will be born tomorrow. I'll hold her in my arms tomorrow. I just pray she doesn't stop moving.

NOVEMBER 21

It's 6 a.m. We've been at the hospital since 3 a.m. Around 2 a.m. I noticed I hadn't been feeling Lily move. She has always been so active and usually moves whenever I want her to. I started to panic. I wasn't able eat or drink to help get her to wake up (because of pre-surgery fasting), and the more I stressed the more I was convinced she was in danger. By the time I woke Justin and we got to the hospital, I started to relax and felt a few little kicks. I still knew I wouldn't be able to rest until she was born, so we went into the hospital and I asked to be monitored until our C-section. Thankfully the nurse was understanding and didn't make me feel like the crazy person I fear I've become. She explained Lily was just sleeping and she'd wake up soon. Sure enough, after a little while, she started kicking and squirming around like usual.

I've been sitting here listening to the steady beating of her heart on the monitor, but even though I know she's okay, I still can't sleep at all. It's so unlike me—I'm generally not an anxious person. But now I feel that there's this unbearable pressure on me to make sure Lily stays alive. Realizing now that it's possible Landon could have been saved if I'd trusted my intuition about what was happening in my body has left me with a terrible feeling. I can't screw up now. I'll gladly be an overly cautious basket-case if that's what it takes to bring home a live baby this time.

Even when I'm not worrying about keeping her alive I'm worrying about what I'm going to do when she's born. How am I supposed to take care of this brand new baby? I don't know a thing about newborns and I'm already so exhausted, hungry and thirsty I can't even think straight.

Everything is happening so quickly but not quickly enough.

NOVEMBER 22

It's hard to believe that only twenty-four hours ago Lily was still inside me. Time has slowed right down, but this time in the best way. Lily's birth was far different from what I'd envisioned or planned but still turned out to be the beautiful, healing and empowering experience I had hoped for. It made me confront my deepest fears and come out stronger than ever. Although it was not the experience I'd originally wanted, it was exactly the experience I needed.

I'd been so sure that avoiding another C-section was the only way I could have a positive birth experience and really heal. But having a C-section with Lily, this time planned and one that I was awake for, ended up being so different from my experience with Landon. By the time we were getting prepped for surgery, our families had arrived and there was so much excitement and joyful anticipation that all of my fears seemed to disappear. The nurses and doctors were amazing. They explained everything that would happen, answered all of our questions and assured me that I would get to see Lily as soon as possible after her birth. They even allowed our birth photographer, Holly, to be in the operating room!

The only painful part of the experience was getting my IV put in because of my veins, which are always so hard to find. During the surgery, my whole body from my neck down was completely numb. Everything felt warm and tingly, and I was actually very relaxed to be lying there, not being able to move a thing—a really blissful *savasana*. When they pulled Lily out of me it felt as though air was being sucked out of my belly. Even though she wasn't making any noise yet, I knew Lily was here.

As soon as Lily was born, my doctor brought her squishy naked body right up next to my face. I couldn't really see her because she was so close, and she still wasn't making much noise, but I could feel her warm body and hear her breathing. She stayed there only for a few seconds before she had to be taken away and checked, but I knew at that moment everything was going to be okay. I would hold my baby girl in my arms soon. My heart nearly exploded with joy.

Lily had to be hooked up to a continuous positive airway pressure (CPAP) machine for about an hour to help with her breathing. (Babies born by C-section sometimes have difficulty because all the fluid doesn't get a chance to clear from their lungs as it does when they are squeezed through the birth canal.) I was so relieved she was here safe and healthy that this hour wait was actually quite joyful, especially in contrast to that agonizing hour or so I waited to be able to see Landon after his birth. Justin and Holly were able to go back and forth between us to keep me updated on how she was doing and show me photos and videos.

When Lily was finally brought to me, I was amazed by how peaceful and calm she was—as though this whole C-section drama and separation from me hadn't even phased her. She rested on my chest for about half an hour, then opened her eyes and looked right at me with her beautiful, deep, dark eyes. She latched onto my breast and started suckling away contently, making the cutest little cooing and squeaking noises. I always imagined that a baby's entry into this world would be frightening for them, but she seemed just so happy to be born and in my arms. (I like to think that maybe Landon has helped prepare her for this big day.) I still look at her and can't believe she is actually here—that this is real life.

Looking back, I'm surprised by the serendipity of the last photo I posted before Lily's arrival. When I posted it, I didn't make the connection, but after her birth it dawned on me that the bridge in the background of the silhouette picture of me doing a warrior pose is the Provencher bridge, the same bridge I photographed and then posted the night before Landon was born. It was fitting for that to be the last photo I posted because of the symbolic significance of a bridge: as a transition, a critical juncture in one's life, a journey from one life to the next, and even birth or rebirth.

The next picture I posted after Landon was born was a picture of my lily flowers. I'd taken the photo just as we were leaving for the hospital. I was sure I was going to use that photo to announce on social media the joyful news of our son's birth. Instead, I ended up using it to announce the most devastating news of our lives. This time, the next photo I posted was a photo of our sweet Lily, sleeping peacefully on my chest. She is more beautiful than I could ever have imagined. It couldn't have been more perfect.

In retrospect, the Brené Brown (*The Gifts of Imperfection*) quotation I posted to go along with the bridge photo before Lily was born also seems remarkably fitting:

> Owning our story can be hard but not nearly as difficult as spending our lives running from it. Embracing our vulnerabilities is risky but not nearly as dangerous as giving up on love and belonging and joy—the experiences that make us the most

vulnerable. Only when we are brave enough to explore the darkness will we discover the infinite power of our light.

At the time, I posted this quotation mainly because I liked the part about embracing darkness, which worked well with the silhouette-style photo. I realize now that it was exactly this—owning my story, my vulnerabilities, my darkness—that brought Lily safely into this world. I'd spent almost a year and a half running from the truth that I'd known something was wrong. I'd known things weren't normal, but I chose to believe that I just needed to relax, that I was healthy, that Landon was healthy and everything would be okay. When I mentioned my symptoms and worries again after his birth, I was still told that any abnormalities would have been detected in our ultrasounds or the placenta, that Landon and I were healthy and that sometimes these things "just happen." So I didn't press further, partly because I wanted to believe them and partly because I didn't believe them but was afraid I wouldn't be able handle the truth—the truth that I could have known … I should have known … and in some ways I DID know, but chose not to do anything. This time was different. I'm different. It was a really hard lesson learned in the absolute worst of ways—but at least now I know. *A mother's intuition is never wrong.*

DECEMBER 4

The results from the bile acid test came back. They were more than quadruple what is considered normal, confirming I did have ICP. Considering the blood was drawn less than twenty-four hours after I first noticed a mild itching, it can be assumed that with Landon my levels were probably extremely high by the time he was born. It's a small miracle he even made it to labour and wasn't a stillbirth as the majority of ICP deaths are.

Getting this official diagnosis wasn't a surprise, as I fully expected this to be the case. In a way it was a relief—at least now I know for certain, and I have an answer about what likely happened to Landon. I did what I thought was necessary to keep Lily safe, and I was right. But it's also hard to make peace with the fact that Landon's death might have been prevented, had I known what I know now—had I trusted that gut feeling that something was wrong and got tested right away. And as positive as Lily's birth experience was, it's a bit disappointing that I'll never get to experience natural childbirth as I hoped I would. If we decide to get pregnant again, I'll probably have ICP, which will mean even more careful monitoring and very likely a C-section delivery by thirty-seven weeks. On the positive side, at least now I know how wonderful a C-section birth can still be and how much easier the recovery from a planned C-section is compared to a crash section. (I felt better the day after Lily's birth than I did two weeks after Landon's, and now almost two weeks later I barely feel like I had surgery!)

As I write this, I keep looking down at Lily curled up snugly on my chest. I still can't believe how perfect she is, how beautiful she is, what a miracle she is. The days leading up to her birth brought a storm of anxiety, fear, doubt and regret, but her safe arrival has been a blessing, a light in the dark like no other. It's said that babies born after loss are "rainbow babies," and I couldn't agree more. As hard as it is to live life without Landon, and as much as I wish Lily could grow up with her brother, I'll always be grateful for my two children— one I carry in my arms, the other I carry in my heart.

EPILOGUE

After sharing Lily's birth story on social media, I received many messages from moms who were diagnosed with ICP after realizing they were experiencing the same symptoms as mine. Many told me they would never have known to get tested had they not read about Lily. Others messaged me saying they had noticed their friend or family member itching and told them about my story and urged them to get information and testing. It makes me proud that not only has Landon's legacy impacted people all over the world in such a profound way, but also it's possible that through sharing his story, and now Lily's birth story, that the lives of other babies have been saved.

THIRTY-NINE WEEKS PREGNANT WITH LANDON

(LEE SPENCE PHOTOGRAPHY)

LANDON AND ME SHORTLY AFTER HE WAS
TAKEN OFF LIFE SUPPORT

(RENEE FRIESEN)

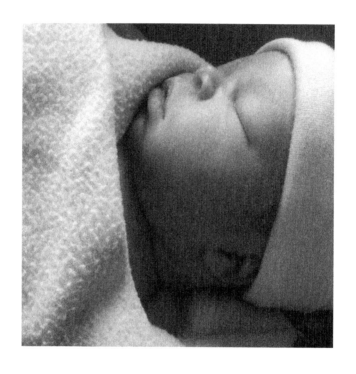

LANDON THE MORNING AFTER HE SURPRISED US BY
STAYING ALIVE THROUGH THE NIGHT

THE MOMENT LANDON TOOK HIS LAST BREATH

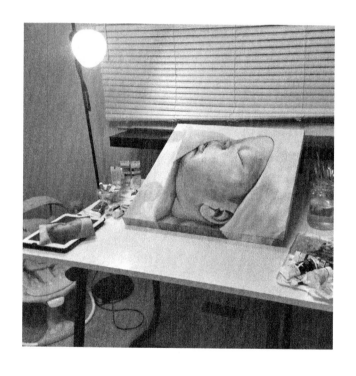

THE PORTRAIT I PAINTED OF LANDON

ME WITH THE BREAST MILK THAT I PUMPED AND DONATED

LANDON'S LEGACY RETREAT 2015

(JENN LAMBERT PHOTOGRAPHY)

IT'S A GIRL!

(JENN LAMBERT PHOTOGRAPHY)

THIRTY-SEVEN WEEKS PREGNANT WITH LILY

(JENN LAMBERT PHOTOGRAPHY)

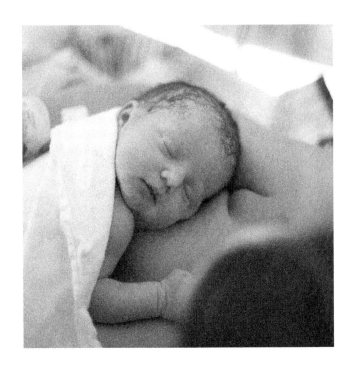

LILY

(HOLLY MICHELLE PHOTOGRAPHY)

ABOUT THE AUTHOR

Amelia Kathryn Barnes is a yoga teacher, retreat facilitator and small business owner. She teaches at Moksha Yoga Winnipeg and is a guide at the yoga and wellness website oneOeight.com. She is also the creator of PranaVidaStyle, a unique line of inspired and Canadian-made yoga apparel. Amelia lives in Winnipeg, Canada with her husband Justin, daughter Lily and their big white mutt Cody.

her websites

http://www.landonslegacyretreat.com/

https://oneoeight.com/guide/amelia-barnes/

https://www.pranavidastyle.com/

CPSIA information can be obtained
at www.ICGtesting.com
Printed in the USA
LVOW04s2050281216
519045LV00004B/9/P